Relative Abundance and Distribution of Fishes and Crayfish at Ash Meadows National Wildlife Refuge, Nye County, Nevada, 2007–08

By G. Gary Scoppettone, Peter Rissler, Danielle Johnson, and Mark Hereford

Open-File Report 2011–1017

U.S. Department of the Interior
U.S. Geological Survey

U.S. Department of the Interior
KEN SALAZAR, Secretary

U.S. Geological Survey
Marcia K. McNutt, Director

U.S. Geological Survey, Reston, Virginia: 2011

For more information on the USGS—the Federal source for science about the Earth, its natural and living resources, natural hazards, and the environment, visit http://www.usgs.gov or call 1-888-ASK-USGS.

For an overview of USGS information products, including maps, imagery, and publications, visit http://www.usgs.gov/pubprod

To order this and other USGS information products, visit http://store.usgs.gov

Suggested citation:
Scoppettone, G.G., Rissler, Peter, Johnson, Danielle, and Hereford, Mark, 2011, Relative abundance and distribution of fishes and crayfish at Ash Meadows National Wildlife Refuge, Nye County, Nevada, 2007–08: U.S. Geological Survey Open-File Report 2011-1017, 56 p.

Contents

Figures

Tables

Conversion Factors

Multiply	By	To obtain
centimeter (cm)	0.3937	inch (in.)
hectare (ha)	2.471	acre
millimeter (mm)	0.03937	inch (in.)
meter (m)	1.094	yard (yd)
liter per minute (L/min)	0.26417	gallon per minute (gal/min)

Temperature in degrees Celsius (°C) may be converted to degrees Fahrenheit (°F) as follows:
°F=(1.8×°C)+32.

Relative Abundance and Distribution of Fishes and Crayfish at Ash Meadows National Wildlife Refuge, Nye County, Nevada, 2007–08

By G. Gary Scoppettone, Peter Rissler, Danielle Johnson, and Mark Hereford

Executive Summary

This study provides baseline data of native and non-native fish populations in Ash Meadows National Wildlife Refuge (NWR), Nye County, Nevada, that can serve as a gauge in native fish enhancement efforts. In support of Carson Slough restoration, comprehensive surveys of Ash Meadows NWR fishes were conducted seasonally from fall 2007 through summer 2008. A total of 853 sampling stations were created using Geographic Information Systems and National Agricultural Imagery Program. In four seasons of sampling, Amargosa pupfish (genus *Cyprinodon*) was captured at 388 of 659 stations. The number of captured Amargosa pupfish ranged from 5,815 (winter 2008) to 8,346 (summer 2008). The greatest success in capturing Amargosa pupfish was in warm water spring-pools with temperature greater than 25°C, headwaters of warm water spring systems, and shallow (depths less than 10 centimeters) grassy marshes. In four seasons of sampling, Ash Meadows speckled dace (*Rhinichthys osculus nevadesis*) was captured at 96 of 659 stations. The number of captured Ash Meadows speckled dace ranged from 1,009 (summer 2008) to 1,552 (winter 2008). The greatest success in capturing Ash Meadows speckled dace was in cool water spring-pools with temperature less than 20°C and in the high flowing water outflows. Among 659 sampling stations within the range of Amargosa pupfish, red swamp crayfish (*Procambarus clarkii*) was collected at 458 stations, western mosquitofish (*Gambusia affinis*) at 374 stations, and sailfin molly (*Poecilia latipinna*) at 128 stations. School Springs was restored during the course of this study. Prior to restoration of School Springs, maximum Warm Springs Amargosa pupfish (*Cyprinodon nevadensis pectoralis*) captured from the six springs of the Warm Springs Complex was 765 (fall 2007). In four seasons of sampling, Warm Springs Amargosa pupfish were captured at 85 of 177 stations. The greatest success in capturing Warm Springs Amargosa pupfish when co-occurring with red swamp crayfish and western mosquitofish was in water with temperature greater than 26°C near the springhead, and in shallow (depths less than 10 centimeters) grassy marshes. Among 177 sampling stations within the range of Warm Springs Amargosa pupfish, red swamp crayfish were collected at 96 stations and western mosquitofish were collected at 49 stations. Removal of convict cichlid (*Amatitlania nigrofasciata*) from Fairbanks Spring was followed by a substantial increase in Ash Meadows Amargosa pupfish (*Cyprinodon nevadensis mionectes*) captures from 910 pre-removal to 3,056 post-removal. Red swamp crayfish was continually removed from

Bradford 1 Spring, which seemed to cause an increase in the speckled dace population. Restoration of Kings Pool and Jackrabbit Springs promoted the success of native fishes with the greatest densities in restored reaches. Ongoing restoration of Carson Slough and its tributaries, as well as control and elimination of invasive species, is expected to increase abundance and distribution of Ash Meadows' native fish populations. Further analysis of data from this study will help determine the habitat characteristic(s) that promote native species and curtail non-native species.

Introduction

The 2007 and 2008 seasonal surveys of this study focused on abundance and distribution of fishes within the boundary of the Ash Meadows National Wildlife Refuge (NWR). This effort was intended to provide baseline information as part of the Carson Slough restoration. Historically, most Ash Meadows NWR spring systems were connected (directly or indirectly; perennially or intermittently) to Carson Slough (Miller, 1948). Thus, slough restoration includes reconnection of tributaries, which in turn necessitates a comprehensive survey of Ash Meadows endangered fish populations to comply with the National Environmental Policy Act (U.S. Environmental Protection Agency, 2010) and Endangered Species Act (U.S. Department of the Interior, 1973). This study is intended to fulfill the requirements of these two Federal acts. The first published Ash Meadows fishes survey was conducted by Miller (1948), who described Warm Springs Amargosa pupfish (*Cyprinodon nevadensis pectoralis*) (CYPE), Ash Meadows Amargosa pupfish (*Cyprinodon nevadensis mionectes*) (CYMI), and revisited the description of the now extinct Ash Meadows poolfish (*Empetrichthys merriami*). Miller (1948) briefly describes the springs these fishes occupied along with cohabitants, native Ash Meadows speckled dace [*Rhinichthys osculus nevadesis* (Hubbs and Deacon, 1964; Miller, 1948)] (RHON) and non-native western mosquitofish (*Gambusia affinis*) (GAAF). Hardy (1979) reported on the relative abundance and distribution of fishes in most the Ash Meadows NWR spring systems, but his observations were qualitative as were those of Threloff (1990). Scoppettone and others (1995) seasonally conducted an abundance and distribution study of Ash Meadows NWR fishes, but did not include all Ash Meadows NWR spring systems. Other publications and reports on distributions pertained to new localities (Miller and Deacon, 1973; Baugh and others, 1986) and publications and reports on abundance typically focused on spring-pools (Williams and Sada, 1985). Because the Ash Meadows NWR's water resources are so extensive, no comprehensive and systematic survey has been completed of Ash Meadows NWR fishes. In this study, we monitored the relative abundance and distribution of fishes and crayfish of the Ash Meadows NWR. Crayfish were included because these fishes seem to negatively affect native fish populations. Each sampling location is described and habitat conditions are quantified.

Background

Native fish abundance and distribution at Ash Meadows have been negatively affected by a long history of spring system alteration, water manipulation, and introduction of non-native aquatic species (Miller, 1948; Pister, 1974; Dudley and Larson, 1976; Soltz and Naiman, 1978; Sada, 1990). Habitat and water manipulation for agriculture and municipal use ceased with the establishment of the Ash Meadows NWR, but eroding irrigation channels, habitat improvement projects, and continued presence of invasive aquatic species caused ongoing changes in native fish populations that masked fluctuations in natural populations (Williams and others, 2001). Documentation of recent human induced habitat alterations was used in the interpretation of our results.

Habitat Alteration and Water Manipulation

Habitat alteration and water manipulation of Ash Meadows springs for agricultural purposes began in the 19th century (Rectangular Survey Plat Map, December 1881 and January 1882), was intensive in the 1970s (Soltz and Naiman, 1978; Sada, 1990; Deacon and Williams, 1991), and ended when the Ash Meadows NWR was established in 1984. By that time, Ash Meadows was incorporated into the National Wildlife Refuge system, many of the springheads had been enlarged, and discharge was conveyed in excavated earthen and concrete ditches. Although native fish habitat had been greatly altered, the virtual halt to diversion of water for irrigation provided fish a more stable environment with water and fish no longer being lost to irrigated fields. Presumably, there was a subsequent increase in the number of Amargosa pupfish (genus *Cyprinodon*) and Ash Meadows speckled dace.

Since 1984 when the Ash Meadow NWR was established, local habitat and water manipulation projects generally focused on enhancement of native fish populations. In the early 1990s, Lower Crystal Marsh was created by breaching the southeastern dike of Horseshoe Reservoir, and was further modified in the 1990s. This action was intended to expand the wetland to benefit Ash Meadows Amargosa pupfish (Threloff, 1990). Dry headwater marshes (water breached unmaintained excavated earthen or concrete irrigation ditches) were created by directing local flow into a stream channel. For example, in 1997, Kings Pool spring-pool was reduced in size to the presumed original size and the meandering stream channel was excavated (Gourley and Ammon, 1997); this action had a positive effect on the Ash Meadows Amargosa pupfish population (Scoppettone and others, 2005). In the mid-1990s, about 70 m of Fairbanks Spring outflow was trenched 300 m downstream of the spring-pool to prevent water from flooding the road. Although inadvertent, this action was presumed to improve Ash Meadows Amargosa pupfish habitat. Restoration also was implemented at Point-of-Rocks Spring in 2001 and at the upper and lower parts of Jackrabbit Spring outflow channel in the summers of 2006 and 2007, respectively. During the course of this study, School Spring was rehabilitated from a series of concrete pools (constructed in the 1970s and 1980s) to a flowing stream with small pools terminating in a marsh.

Non-Native Species

The introduction of several non-native species has contributed to the decline of Ash Meadows native fish (Williams and Deacon, 1986; Sada, 1990; Kennedy and others, 2006). Mosquitofish was established by the 1930s and was the first reported introduction of a non-native species (Miller, 1948). Sailfin molly (*Poecilia latipinna*) (POLA) was established by the early 1960s (La Rivers, 1962; Deacon and others, 1964; Hubbs and Deacon, 1964); several other tropical fishes appeared in Ash Meadows waters about the same time, but these tropical fishes did not establish a reproductive population (Soltz and Naiman, 1978). A population of the tropical convict cichlid (*Archocentrus nigrofasciatus*) (ARNI) was discovered in Fairbanks spring-pool in October 2001 (Shawn Goodchild, U.S. Fish and Wildlife Service, oral commun., 2001). Largemouth bass (*Micropterus salmoides*) (MISA) has been present in the Ash Meadows spring systems since the 1960s (Williams and Deacon, 1986; Sada, 1990) and since 1995, have established in Point-of-Rocks, King's Pool, Forest, Big, Bradford 2, and Crystal Springs. Green sunfish (*Lepomis cyanellus*) (LECY) appeared in Crystal Reservoir in the 1990s, and in Bradford 2 Spring by 2001 (Leavy and others, 2004). A reproductive population of black bullhead (*Ameiurus melas*) (AMME) has occupied Davis Spring; chemical removal of this population was attempted in the1990s and again in July 2008 (Darrick Weissenfluh, Ash Meadows National Wildlife Refuge, oral commun., 2008).

Several largemouth bass in Big Spring and an apparent invasion of bass and green sunfish into the inflow of Crystal Reservoir were documented during this study. In January 2008, convict cichlids were chemically removed from Fairbanks Spring (Darrick Weissenfluh, Ash Meadows National Wildlife Refuge, oral commun., 2008). Red swamp crayfish (*Procambarus clarkii*) (PRCL) and American bullfrog (*Lithobates catesbeiana*) (LICA) have been established since the early 1960s (Sada, 1990). The exact date of introduction is unknown.

Materials and Methods

We used Geographic Information Systems (GIS) using the National Agricultural Imagery Program (NAIP) to trace stream channels and to determine locations of sampling stations. A total of 853 sampling locations were established, but the number of locations with water sufficiently deep to trap fish ranged from 781 in fall 2007 to 631 in summer 2008 (fig. 1). North American Datum (NAD) 83 decimal degrees of longitude and latitude of each station were downloaded into Garmin Global Positioning System (GPS) units. These units typically are accurate within a 2 m radius of a specific station. GIS also was used to illustrate seasonal distribution and relative abundance of fishes in each spring system. The data collected during these seasonal sampling periods were used to develop species specific GIS maps, which display range and densities. Where it was feasible (relatively long outflows and some marshes), a fixed kernel methodology was used (Worton, 1987) to focus on areas of greatest concentration of fish population. A 95 percent kernel was the minimum area in which 95 percent of the population occupied, and 50 percent kernel was the minimum area in which 50 percent of the population occupied. ArcView GIS and Animal Movement Extension (Hooge and Eichenlaub, 1997) were used to estimate kernel densities.

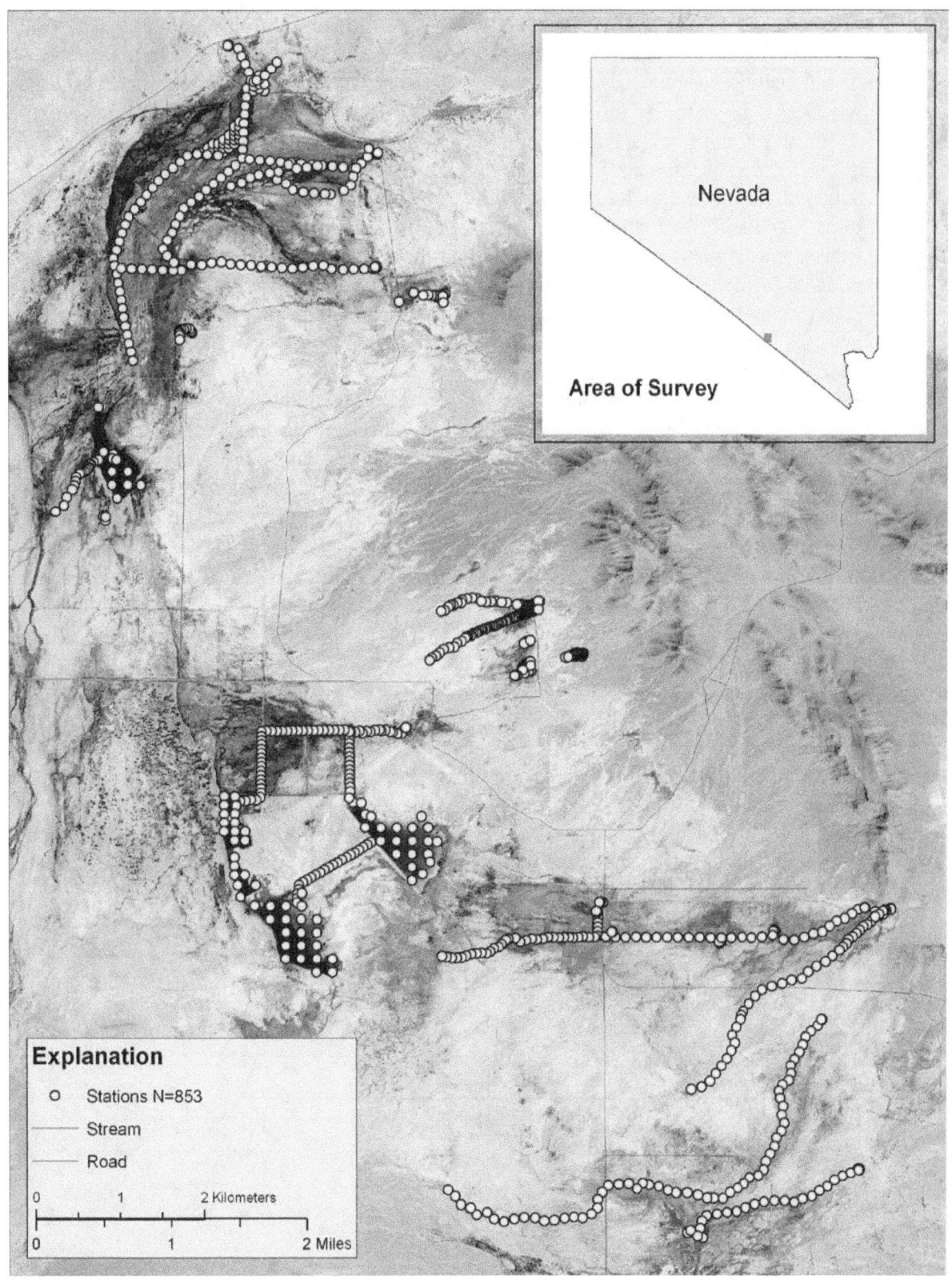

Figure 1. Aerial photograph of Ash Meadows National Wildlife Refuge showing 853 potential sampling stations, Nye County, Nevada.

Most traps were set in the afternoon and pulled the following morning. Shorter sets, placed in the morning and pulled 3–9.5 hours later, were used in areas with high fish densities, high crayfish densities, spring pools, and areas of relatively warm water with temperatures greater then 29°C to prevent fish mortality. Each station was sampled for all four seasons unless precluded by restoration projects, water level too low for successful fish capture, or water velocity to fast for traps to remain. Small minnow traps (90 mm in diameter) were fabricated to sample shallow areas and were effective in depths to 60 mm. Entries for standard and fabricated minnow traps was 20 mm in diameter, trap walls were made up of a 3.3 mm mesh. Standard minnow traps allow fish entry from two sides and fabricated traps allow fish entry from one side. Traps were baited with dry dog food. At each station, fish were identified to species, counted, and 10–20 individuals were randomly selected and measured to fork length (FL). The capture gear and seasonal effort used at each system are presented in the first table of each of the three regional appendixes (appendixes A–C).

Water-quality data (pH, temperature, dissolved oxygen, conductivity, and depth) were collected at each station using HydroLab MS5 or other equivalent water-sampling equipment. Water depth was measured at or near the site of minnow trap placement where possible. Flow was measured in fall 2009 with a Marsh McBirney Model 201 portable water current meter. Vegetation and substrate surveys were completed in spring 2008 and winter 2009, and were comprised of species-specific cover estimates of canopy, aquatic surface, and subsurface aquatic vegetation densities.

We used Program ArcGIS 9.3's ArcHydro Tools 9 to illustrate the relation of Ash Meadows spring outflows to historical Carson Slough and 3- and 10-m Digital Elevation Models (DEM) as a base layer for historical watercourse analysis (fig. 2). Alternate historical flows were modeled in cases where terrain structures could cause water to flow in multiple directions. The current and modeled historical outflows shown in figure 2 will aid in interpretation of fish and crayfish distribution.

Relative abundance and distribution are illustrated using three methods–(1) total fish captured in each system and major habitat type (springhead, spring-pool, outflow, marsh, and reservoir) is shown by season in tabular form, (2) distribution and abundance (combined seasonal data to streamline this report) are presented using GIS-generated maps, and (3) kernel densities are estimated based on selected systems for describing seasonal distribution. For ease of reporting, Ash Meadows NWR spring systems were divided into three different regions: northern springs, Warm Springs Complex, and southern springs.

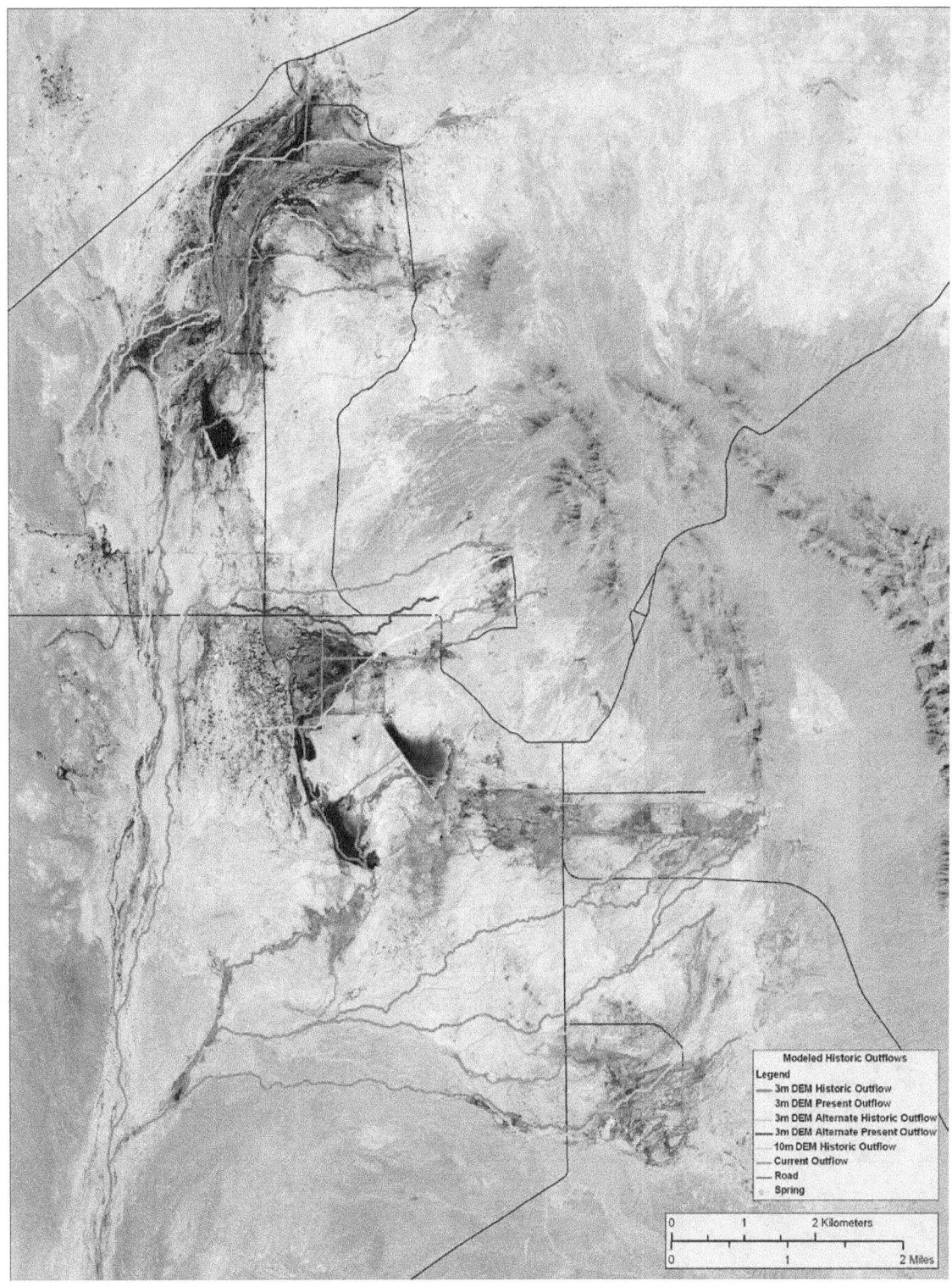

Figure 2. Aerial photograph of Ash Meadows National Wildlife Refuge showing spring outflows and modeled historical outflows using 3- and 10-meter Digital Elevation Models (DEM) of Ash Meadows National Wildlife Refuge, Nevada.

Results

Northern Springs

The greatest Ash Meadows Amargosa pupfish density in Fairbanks, Rogers, and Longstreet Springs was in the spring-pool, as was true of most Ash Meadows large warm water spring systems (fig. 3, table 1). Total capture of Ash Meadows Amargosa pupfish from Rogers and Longstreet Springs was greater in the spring-pool than the entire outflow. Longstreet Spring was the only northern spring harboring sailfin molly, and total number and catch rate were greatest in the spring-pool (appendix A: table A1, fig. A2). The greatest number of bullfrog tadpole captures was from Rogers Spring, and most were from the spring-pool in each of the four seasonal surveys.

Western mosquitofish were the only minnow trap captures from Soda Spring (fall 2007); crayfish were captured in all four seasonal surveys (table 1, appendix A: figs. A1 and A4). Our captures suggest Cold Spring probably is the only Ash Meadows spring where Ash Meadows Amargosa pupfish is not sympatric with mosquitofish.

After chemical removal of convict cichlids and mosquitofish in Fairbanks spring-pool and part of the outflow in January 2008, Ash Meadows pupfish captures markedly increased. In Fairbanks spring-pool, captures per trap almost doubled from a total capture of 453 Ash Meadows Amargosa pupfish (75.5 / trap) in fall 2007 to 821 captures (136.8 / trap) in summer 2008 (appendix A: table A1). Prior to treatment, convict cichlids were concentrated in the upper 300 m of the stream but several were captured as far as 1,500 m downstream (appendix A: fig. A3). Water temperatures at the time of capture ranged from 25.5 to 27.5°C.

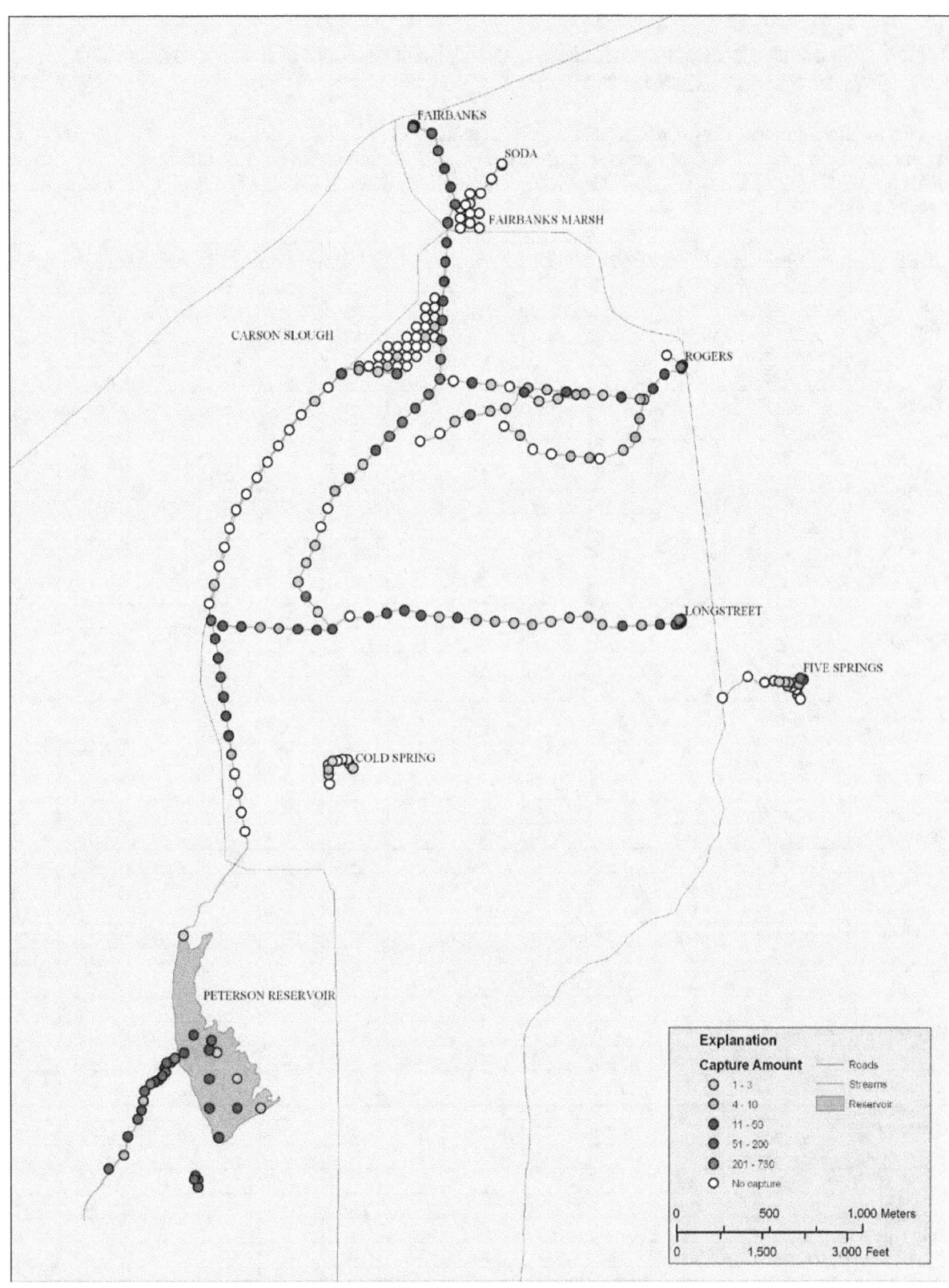

Figure 3. Relative abundance and distribution of Ash Meadows Amargosa pupfish in the northern springs, Ash Meadows National Wildlife Refuge, Nevada, fall 2007–summer 2008.

Table 1. Seasonal catches of fishes, bullfrogs, and crayfish at the northern springs of the Ash Meadows National Wildlife Refuge, Nevada, fall 2007–summer 2008.

[Spring locations are shown in figures 1 and 2. CYMI, Ash Meadows Amargosa pupfish; CYPE, Warm Springs Amargosa pupfish; RHON, Ash Meadows speckled dace; GAAF, Mosquitofish; POLA, Sailfin Molly; LECY, Green Sunfish; MISA, Largemouth Bass; ARNI, Convict Cichlid; AMME, Black Bullhead; LICA, Bull Frog; PRCL, Red Swamp Crayfish]

System	Season	CYMI	CYPE	RHON	GAAF	POLA	LECY	MISA	ARNI	AMME	LICA	PRCL
Fairbanks spring-pool	Fall 07	453	–	–	1	–	–	–	50	–	5	4
	Winter 08	581	–	–	–	–	–	–	–	–	–	18
	Spring 08	358	–	–	–	–	–	–	–	–	–	21
	Summer 08	821	–	–	–	–	–	–	–	–	–	35
Fairbanks stream	Fall 07	457	–	–	200	–	–	–	72	–	4	144
	Winter 08	149	–	–	–	–	–	–	–	–	–	131
	Spring 08	284	–	–	2	–	–	–	–	–	7	196
	Summer 08	2235	–	–	45	–	–	–	–	–	–	295
Fairbanks marsh	Fall 07	–	–	–	–	–	–	–	–	–	–	2
	Winter 08	–	–	–	–	–	–	–	–	–	–	–
	Spring 08	–	–	–	–	–	–	–	–	–	–	6
Carson marsh	Fall 07	4	–	–	11	–	–	–	–	–	–	50
Soda spring-pool	Fall 07	–	–	–	8	–	–	–	–	–	–	12
	Winter 08	–	–	–	–	–	–	–	–	–	–	18
	Spring 08	–	–	–	–	–	–	–	–	–	–	13
	Summer 08	–	–	–	–	–	–	–	–	–	–	16
Soda stream	Fall 07	–	–	–	3	–	–	–	–	–	–	12
	Winter 08	–	–	–	–	–	–	–	–	–	–	5
	Spring 08	–	–	–	–	–	–	–	–	–	–	8
	Summer 08	–	–	–	–	–	–	–	–	–	–	3
Rogers spring-pool	Fall 07	410	–	–	42	–	–	–	–	–	12	12
	Winter 08	466	–	–	69	–	–	–	–	–	29	27
	Spring 08	340	–	–	39	–	–	–	–	–	9	31
	Summer 08	341	–	–	248	–	–	–	–	–	2	32
Rogers stream	Fall 07	44	–	–	485	–	–	–	–	–	1	214
	Winter 08	59	–	–	123	–	–	–	–	–	1	227
	Spring 08	149	–	–	250	–	–	–	–	–	2	184
	Summer 08	60	–	–	919	–	–	–	–	–	–	144
Longstreet spring-pool	Fall 07	546	–	–	56	53	–	–	–	–	–	17
	Winter 08	332	–	–	36	19	–	–	–	–	–	23
	Spring 08	353	–	–	1	45	–	–	–	–	–	23
	Summer 08	458	–	–	80	133	–	–	–	–	–	69
Longstreet stream	Fall 07	3	–	–	7	2	–	–	–	–	–	33
	Winter 08	22	–	–	6	1	–	–	–	–	–	22
	Spring 08	95	–	–	39	5	–	–	–	–	–	53
	Summer 08	98	–	–	73	4	–	–	–	–	–	68
Five Springs spring-pool	Fall 07	32	–	–	–	–	–	–	–	–	–	2
	Winter 08	21	–	–	9	–	–	–	–	–	–	1
	Spring 08	23	–	–	5	–	–	–	–	–	–	5
	Summer 08	21	–	–	3	–	–	–	–	–	–	–
Five Springs stream	Fall 07	4	–	–	13	–	–	–	–	–	–	7
	Winter 08	3	–	–	57	–	–	–	–	–	–	20
	Spring 08	13	–	–	75	–	–	–	–	–	–	9
	Summer 08	46	–	–	68	–	–	–	–	–	–	41

Table 1. Seasonal catches of fishes, bullfrogs, and crayfish at the northern springs of the Ash Meadows National Wildlife Refuge, Nevada, fall 2007–summer 2008.—Continued

System	Season	CYMI	CYPE	RHON	GAAF	POLA	LECY	MISA	ARNI	AMME	LICA	PRCL
Peterson reservoir	Fall 07	44	–	–	2	–	–	–	–	–	–	3
	Winter 08	2	–	–	–	–	–	–	–	–	–	1
	Spring 08	12	–	–	–	–	–	–	–	–	–	4
	Summer 08	157	–	–	95	–	–	–	–	–	–	3
Peterson stream	Fall 07	351	–	–	75	–	–	–	–	–	–	1
	Winter 08	108	–	–	5	–	–	–	–	–	–	28
	Spring 08	861	–	–	11	–	–	–	–	–	–	8
	Summer 08	509	–	–	993	–	–	–	–	–	–	20
Cold spring-pool	Fall 07	–	–	–	–	–	–	–	–	–	–	17
	Winter 08	–	–	–	–	–	–	–	–	–	–	45
	Spring 08	–	–	–	–	–	–	–	–	–	–	32
	Summer 08	–	–	–	–	–	–	–	–	–	–	33
Cold pool	Fall 07	–	–	–	–	–	–	–	–	–	–	25
	Winter 08	–	–	–	–	–	–	–	–	–	–	32
	Spring 08	–	–	–	–	–	–	–	–	–	–	18
	Summer 08	–	–	–	–	–	–	–	–	–	–	16
Cold stream	Fall 07	3	–	–	–	–	–	–	–	–	–	39
	Winter 08	–	–	–	–	–	–	–	–	–	–	113
	Spring 08	4	–	–	–	–	–	–	–	–	–	54
	Summer 08	–	–	–	–	–	–	–	–	–	–	68

Soda spring-pool water temperatures were cooler and fluctuated more than Fairbanks and Rogers spring-pools. Temperatures ranged from 19.1°C (winter 2008) to 26.2°C (summer 2008) in Soda, 26.9 to 28.5°C in Fairbanks, and 28.4 to 29.7°C in Rogers Springs. Longstreet spring-pool was slightly warmer than Soda spring-pool ranging from 19.9 to 28.8°C, but also displayed a rather broad seasonal fluctuation. Five Springs and Cold Spring, like Soda Spring, have relatively low discharge (<300 L/min) (Dudley and Larson, 1976). Five Springs are at the highest elevation (715 m) and were the warmest (32–34°C). Cold Spring was the coolest (18°C) of the northern springs. Ash Meadows Amargosa pupfish have been observed in Five Springs and Cold Spring. Five Springs captures were concentrated near the upper reaches and western mosquitofish was predominantly captured, although no mosquitofish were captured from Cold Spring.

Warm Springs Complex

When this study began in fall 2007, four of the six springs of the Warm Springs Complex harbored crayfish and mosquitofish (North Indian, South Indian, South Scruggs, and School Springs). No Warm Springs Amargosa pupfish were captured or observed in South Indian Spring. In North Indian Spring, Warm Springs Amargosa pupfish captures ranged from 79 (fall 2007) to 34 (winter 2008), but were present only in the first 100 m of the outflow (fig. 4, table 2). Mosquitofish and crayfish were captured at all South Indian Spring trapping stations, although Warm Springs Amargosa pupfish were more localized (appendix B: table B1, figs. B1 and B2).

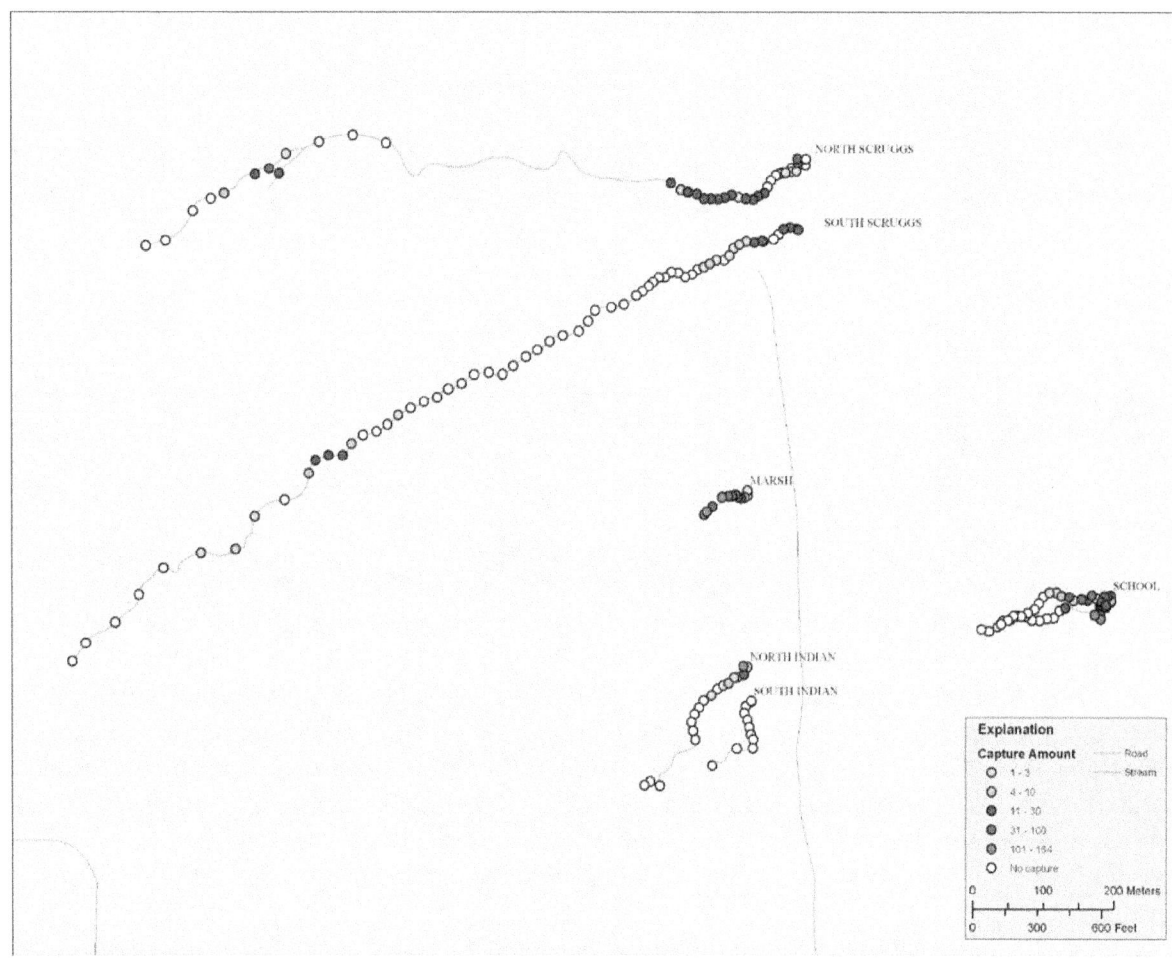

Figure 4. Relative abundance and distribution of Warm Springs Amargosa pupfish in the Warm Springs Complex, Ash Meadows National Wildlife Refuge, Nevada, fall 2007–summer 2008.

Table 2. Seasonal catches of fishes, bullfrogs, and crayfish at the Warm Springs Complex of the Ash Meadows NWR, Nevada, fall 2007–summer 2008.

[Spring locations are shown in figures 1 and 2. CYMI, Ash Meadows Amargosa pupfish; CYPE, Warm Springs Amargosa pupfish; RHON, Ash Meadows speckled dace; GAAF, Mosquitofish; POLA, Sailfin Molly; LECY, Green Sunfish; MISA, Largemouth Bass; ARNI, Convict Cichlid; AMME, Black Bullhead; LICA, Bull Frog; PRCL, Red Swamp Crayfish]

System	Season	CYMI	CYPE	RHON	GAAF	POLA	LECY	MISA	ARNI	AMME	LICA	PRCL
North Scruggs spring-pool	Fall 07	–	–	–	–	–	–	–	–	–	–	–
	Winter 08	–	–	–	–	–	–	–	–	–	–	–
	Spring 08	–	7	–	–	–	–	–	–	–	–	–
	Summer 08	–	16	–	–	–	–	–	–	–	–	–
North Scruggs stream	Fall 07	–	86	–	–	–	–	–	–	–	–	–
	Winter 08	–	84	–	–	–	–	–	–	–	–	–
	Spring 08	–	81	–	–	–	–	–	–	–	–	–
	Summer 08	–	115	–	–	–	–	–	–	–	–	–
South Scruggs spring-pool	Fall 07	–	17	–	–	–	–	–	–	–	–	6
	Winter 08	–	–	–	–	–	–	–	–	–	–	1
	Spring 08	–	4	–	–	–	–	–	–	–	–	4
	Summer 08	–	2	–	–	–	–	–	–	–	–	9
South Scruggs stream	Fall 07	–	40	–	16	–	–	–	–	–	–	157
	Winter 08	–	57	–	14	–	–	–	–	–	–	131
	Spring 08	–	52	–	37	–	–	–	–	–	–	119
	Summer 08	–	51	–	21	–	–	–	–	–	–	103
Marsh spring-pool	Fall 07	–	–	–	–	–	–	–	–	–	–	–
	Winter 08	–	–	–	–	–	–	–	–	–	–	–
	Spring 08	–	1	–	–	–	–	–	–	–	–	–
	Summer 08	–	–	–	–	–	–	–	–	–	–	–
Marsh stream	Fall 07	–	168	–	–	–	–	–	–	–	–	–
	Winter 08	–	171	–	–	–	–	–	–	–	–	–
	Spring 08	–	141	–	–	–	–	–	–	–	–	–
	Summer 08	–	152	–	–	–	–	–	–	–	–	–
North Indian spring-pool	Fall 07	–	–	–	–	–	–	–	–	–	–	3
	Winter 08	–	1	–	–	–	–	–	–	–	–	4
	Spring 08	–	1	–	–	–	–	–	–	–	–	–
	Summer 08	–	1	–	–	–	–	–	–	–	–	3
North Indian stream	Fall 07	–	79	–	62	–	–	–	–	–	–	55
	Winter 08	–	34	–	17	–	–	–	–	–	2	34
	Spring 08	–	35	–	15	–	–	–	–	–	–	28
	Summer 08	–	32	–	4	–	–	–	–	–	–	23
South Indian stream	Fall 07	–	–	–	22	–	–	–	–	–	–	15
	Winter 08	–	–	–	2	–	–	–	–	–	–	9
	Spring 08	–	–	–	3	–	–	–	–	–	–	4
	Summer 08	–	–	–	3	–	–	–	–	–	–	5
School spring-pool	Fall 07	–	19	–	3	–	–	–	–	–	–	4
	Winter 08	–	4	–	–	–	–	–	–	–	–	–
	Summer 08	–	6	–	–	–	–	–	–	–	–	–
School ponds	Fall 07	–	294	–	50	–	–	–	–	–	–	21
	Winter 08	–	267	–	45	–	–	–	–	–	–	3
School stream	Fall 07	–	62	–	40	–	–	–	–	–	–	41
	Winter 08	–	116	–	24	–	–	–	–	–	–	43
	Summer 08	–	177	–	–	–	–	–	–	–	–	–

South Scruggs and North Scruggs springs have the longest outflows of the Warm Springs Complex. Warm Springs Amargosa pupfish in South Scruggs Spring was localized in distribution, as demonstrated by kernel density estimation (fig. 5). Most captures were within 150 m of the springhead and then none until about 800 m from the springhead (fig. 4). Mosquitofish rarely overlapped Warm Springs Amargosa pupfish and the greatest density of mosquitofish was in the reach with virtually no Warm Springs Amargosa pupfish captures (appendix B: table B1, fig. B1). Crayfish had the widest distribution among the three species, and almost completely overlapped with Warm Springs Amargosa pupfish and mosquitofish. Although the widest distribution of crayfish was in South Scruggs and North Indian Springs, catch per trap and total captures typically were higher for Warm Springs Amargosa pupfish than crayfish in most seasons. We did not weigh captures, but crayfish biomass seemed to exceed that of Warm Springs Amargosa pupfish.

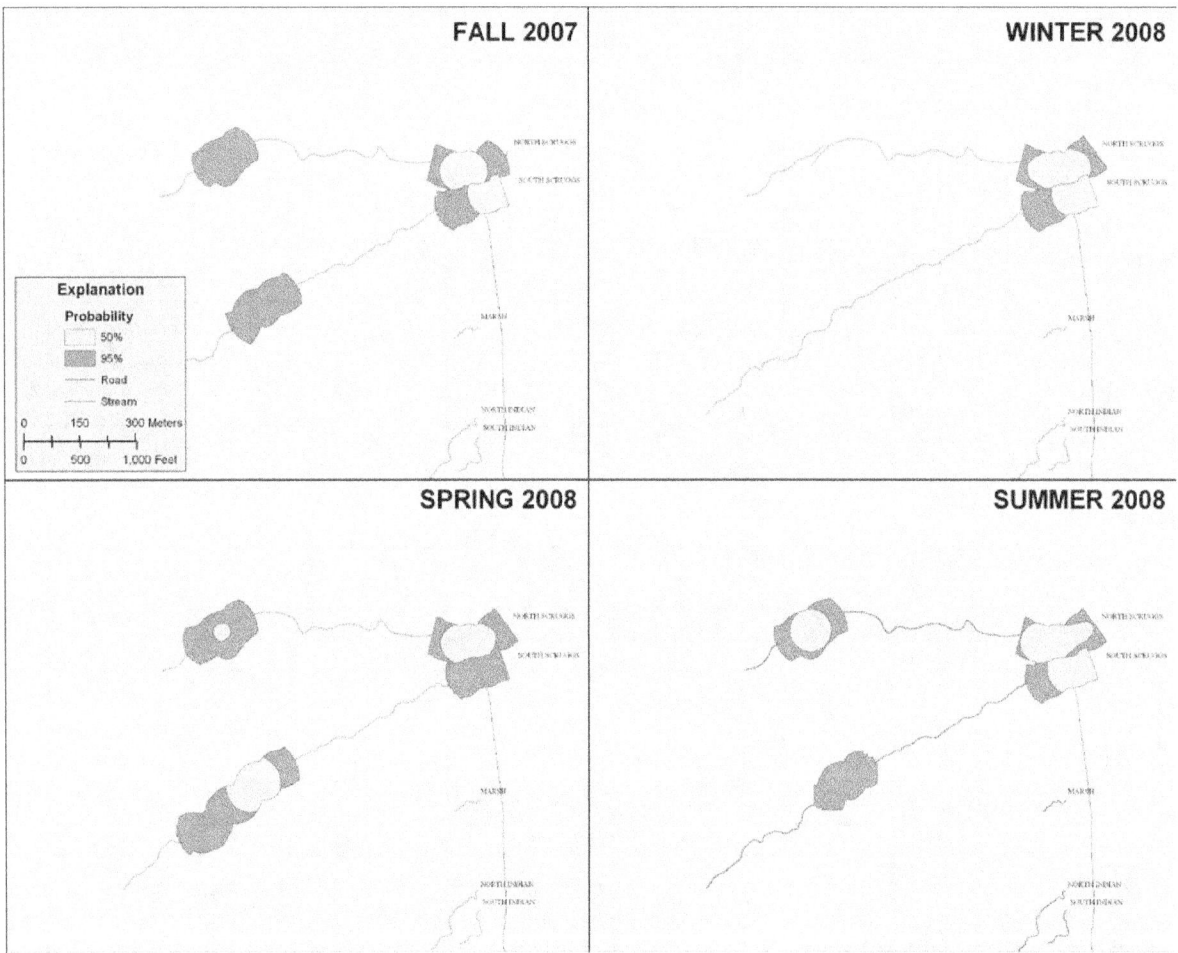

Figure 5. Kernel density estimations (50 and 95 percent probability) of Warm Springs Amargosa pupfish in the Warm Springs Complex, Ash Meadows National Wildlife Refuge, Nevada, fall 2007–summer 2008.

Total catches and catch per trap generally were high in spring systems without crayfish and mosquitofish. Much of North Scruggs Spring was on private property at the time of our surveys and was not sampled. Marsh Spring had the shortest outflow, did not harbor non-native fish or crayfish, and its lower reach has an artificially formed marsh, which provides substantial Warm Springs Amargosa pupfish habitat (and accounted for most captures).

During this study, School Springs was under restoration, including the eradication of mosquitofish and crayfish and redirection of spring outflow. We sampled the spring system in fall 2007 and winter 2008 prior to restoration and then in summer 2008 after restoration. Crayfish and mosquitofish had been introduced into School Springs soon after 2000 (Shawn Goodchild, U.S. Fish and Wildlife Service, oral commun., 2000). Even after these introductions, School Springs had the highest Warm Springs Amargosa pupfish capture rate. Fish were concentrated in the deep concrete pools that were created to promote Warm Springs Amargosa pupfish in School Springs. There have been concerted efforts to remove all non-native fish from these artificial pools. Our sampling of the restored School Springs confirms that crayfish and mosquitofish were eradicated.

Southern Springs

Crystal Spring is the largest volume spring in Ash Meadows NWR and its outflow supports the greatest surface area of wetlands, which consists of a spring-pool, outflow, concrete channels, Crystal Reservoir, Horseshoe Reservoir, and Crystal Marsh. Within this extensive system, Ash Meadows Amargosa pupfish captures were greatest in the spring-pool and streams (fig. 6). Relatively few captures were from reservoir and marsh habitats, especially Crystal Reservoir and Crystal Marsh. These areas were occupied by largemouth bass and green sunfish. Where centrarchids occurred, Ash Meadows Amargosa pupfish, crayfish, and mosquitofish were scarce. Ash Meadows Amargosa pupfish was the predominant species captured in Crystal spring-pool and outflow, followed by crayfish, mosquitofish, and sailfin molly (table 3). Like Ash Meadows Amargosa pupfish, sailfin molly and crayfish were captured with high frequently in the upper 800 m of the outflow, and with high frequency in Horseshoe Marsh (appendix C: figs. C2 and C5).

Kings Pool spring-pool, like the other Ash Meadows NWR warm water spring-pools, had substantially greater Ash Meadows Amargosa pupfish captures per trap compared to its outflow. Highest spring-pool capture was in fall 2007 when 838 Ash Meadows Amargosa pupfish were captured with a success rate of 139.7 captures per trap (table 3, appendix C: table C1). Ash Meadows Amargosa pupfish were observed along the entire course of Kings Pool outflow; the greatest concentration of Ash Meadows Amargosa pupfish was within 500 m of the spring-pool (fig. 6). Greatest concentrations of crayfish were observed 500 m downstream of the spring-pool (appendix C: fig. C5). Although somewhat localized in distribution, more Ash Meadows Amargosa pupfish were captured than non-native fish (table 3).

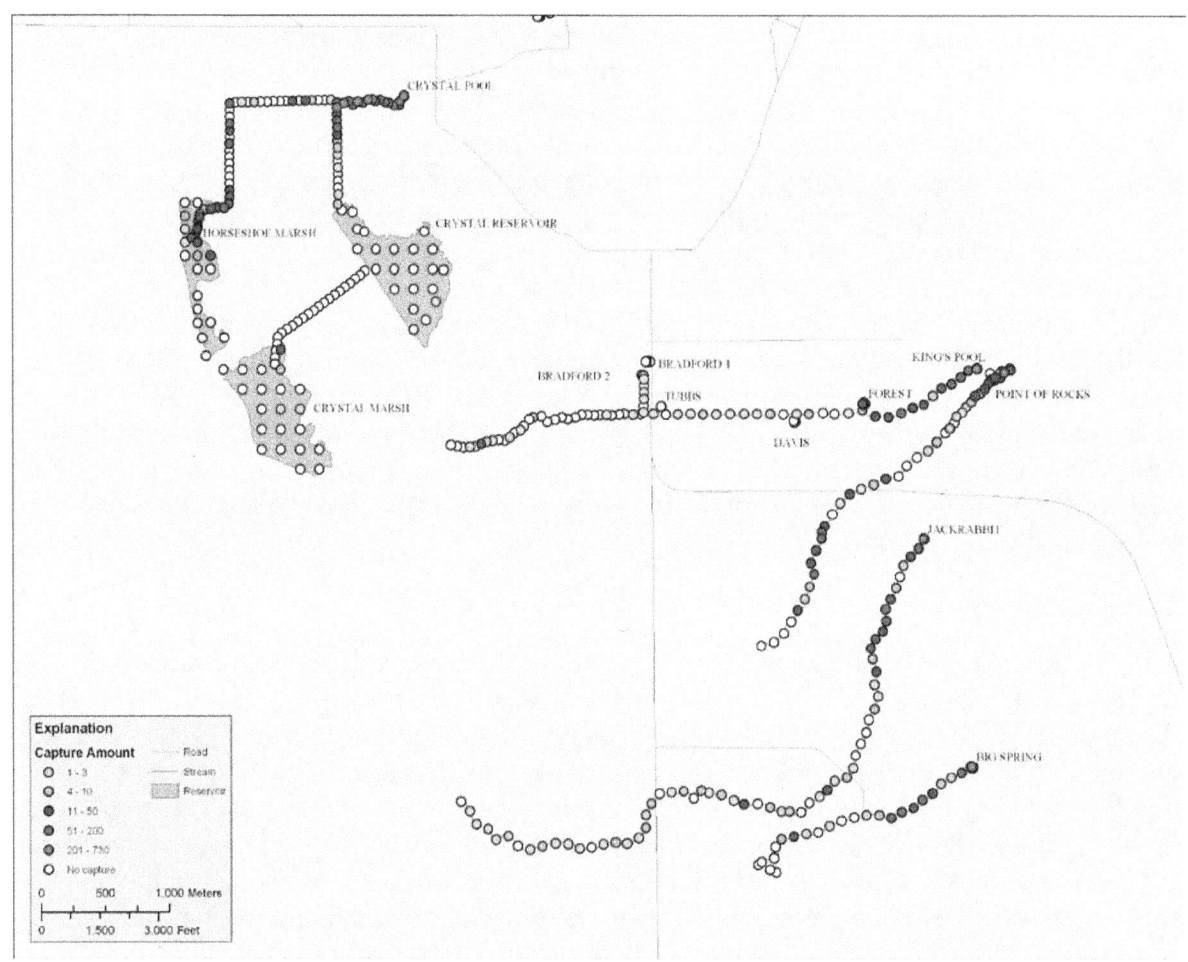

Figure 6. Relative abundance and distribution of Ash Meadows Amargosa pupfish in the southern springs, Ash Meadows National Wildlife Refuge, Nevada, fall 2007–summer 2008.

Table 3. Seasonal catches of fishes, bullfrogs, and crayfish at the southern springs of the Ash Meadows National Wildlife Refuge, Nevada, fall 2007–summer 2008.

[Spring locations are shown in figures 1 and 2. CYMI, Ash Meadows Amargosa pupfish; CYPE, Warm Springs Amargosa pupfish; RHON, Ash Meadows speckled dace; GAAF, Mosquitofish; POLA, Sailfin Molly; LECY, Green Sunfish; MISA, Largemouth Bass; ARNI, Convict Cichlid; AMME, Black Bullhead; LICA, Bull Frog; PRCL, Red Swamp Crayfish]

System	Season	CYMI	CYPE	RHON	GAAF	POLA	LECY	MISA	ARNI	AMME	LICA	PRCL
Crystal spring-pool	Fall 07	319	–	–	66	1	–	–	–	–	–	70
	Winter 08	594	–	–	31	–	–	–	–	–	–	68
	Spring 08	564	–	–	21	2	–	–	–	–	–	24
	Summer 08	554	–	–	27	–	–	–	–	–	–	34
Crystal stream	Fall 07	1,423	–	–	339	105	–	–	–	–	–	609
	Winter 08	1,099	–	–	318	17	–	–	–	–	–	639
	Spring 08	646	–	–	190	11	–	–	–	–	–	402
	Summer 08	958	–	–	242	3	–	–	–	–	–	605
Crystal reservoir	Fall 07	1	–	–	–	–	386	3	–	–	–	–
	Winter 08	–	–	–	–	–	4	–	–	–	–	–
	Spring 08	5	–	–	–	–	9	5	–	–	–	–
	Summer 08	–	–	–	–	–	77	–	–	–	–	–
Crystal stream	Fall 07	–	–	–	1	–	10	–	–	–	–	1
	Winter 08	–	–	–	–	–	5	–	–	–	–	1
Crystal marsh	Fall 07	24	–	–	66	–	26	–	–	–	–	3
	Winter 08	14	–	–	5	–	4	–	–	–	–	1
	Spring 08	6	–	–	–	–	27	16	–	–	–	3
	Summer 08	4	–	–	4	–	41	1	–	–	–	–
Horseshoe marsh	Fall 07	17	–	–	97	54	–	–	–	–	1	210
	Winter 08	27	–	–	18	34	1	–	–	–	11	81
	Spring 08	72	–	–	16	19	5	–	–	–	2	174
	Summer 08	12	–	–	437	44	–	–	–	–	37	162
Kings Pool spring-pool	Fall 07	838	–	–	4	–	–	–	–	–	–	–
	Winter 08	531	–	–	16	–	–	–	–	–	–	–
	Spring 08	653	–	–	1	–	–	–	–	–	–	–
	Summer 08	701	–	–	2	–	–	–	–	–	–	–
Kings Pool stream	Fall 07	179	–	1	57	29	–	–	–	–	–	80
	Winter 08	106	–	–	35	12	–	–	–	–	–	47
	Spring 08	170	–	–	29	29	–	–	–	–	–	78
	Summer 08	157	–	–	74	41	–	–	–	–	–	104
Point of Rocks stream	Fall 07	237	–	–	29	5	–	–	–	–	–	196
	Winter 08	179	–	5	91	7	–	–	–	–	1	91
	Spring 08	227	–	2	49	6	–	–	–	–	–	148
	Summer 08	234	–	–	119	3	–	–	–	–	–	198
Bradford 1 spring-pool	Fall 07	–	–	615	125	–	–	–	–	–	–	37
	Winter 08	–	–	694	447	–	–	–	–	–	–	15
	Spring 08	–	–	383	51	–	–	–	–	–	–	29
	Summer 08	–	–	265	334	1	–	–	–	–	–	29
Bradford 1 stream	Fall 07	–	–	80	93	–	–	–	–	–	–	30
	Winter 08	–	–	77	78	–	–	–	–	–	–	18
	Spring 08	–	–	–	261	–	–	–	–	–	–	13
	Summer 08	–	–	33	692	–	–	–	–	–	–	26
Bradford 2 spring-pool	Fall 07	–	–	31	358	–	–	–	–	–	–	153
	Winter 08	–	–	9	390	141	–	–	–	–	–	52
	Spring 08	–	–	–	–	–	–	–	–	–	1	95
	Summer 08	–	–	2	31	–	–	–	–	–	–	40

Table 3. Seasonal catches of fishes, bullfrogs, and crayfish at the southern springs of the Ash Meadows National Wildlife Refuge, Nevada, fall 2007–summer 2008.—Continued.

System	Season	CYMI	CYPE	RHON	GAAF	POLA	LECY	MISA	ARNI	AMME	LICA	PRCL
Bradford 2 stream	Fall 07	15	–	95	163	22	–	–	–	–	1	141
	Winter 08	3	–	94	130	14	–	–	–	–	1	100
	Spring 08	14	–	79	88	1	–	–	–	–	2	85
	Summer 08	5	–	78	123	4	–	–	–	–	–	120
Forest spring-pool	Fall 07	1	–	5	462	9	–	–	–	–	–	140
	Winter 08	2	–	7	397	15	–	–	–	–	–	45
	Spring 08	55	–	7	287	1	–	–	–	–	–	152
	Summer 08	42	–	1	415	4	–	–	–	–	–	140
Tubbs spring-pool	Fall 07	–	–	–	–	–	–	–	–	–	4	6
	Winter 08	–	–	–	–	–	–	–	–	–	–	16
	Spring 08	–	–	–	–	–	–	–	–	–	2	49
	Summer 08	–	–	–	–	–	–	–	–	–	8	51
Davis spring-pool	Fall 07	–	–	–	119	–	–	–	–	8	–	5
	Winter 08	–	–	–	1	–	–	–	–	–	–	4
	Spring 08	–	–	–	359	–	–	–	–	2	–	19
	Summer 08	–	–	–	–	–	–	–	–	–	–	11
Jackrabbit spring-pool	Fall 07	786	–	19	55	69	–	–	–	–	–	25
	Winter 08	726	–	21	52	35	–	–	–	–	–	24
	Spring 08	761	–	31	1	75	–	–	–	–	–	19
	Summer 08	512	–	23	28	32	–	–	–	–	–	43
Jackrabbit stream	Fall 07	79	–	510	121	36	–	–	–	–	–	291
	Winter 08	169	–	645	56	3	–	–	–	–	–	295
	Spring 08	175	–	652	91	8	–	–	–	–	1	288
	Summer 08	147	–	607	333	11	–	–	–	–	–	461
Big Spring spring-pool	Fall 07	157	–	–	2	40	–	–	–	–	–	–
	Winter 08	416	–	–	13	9	–	–	–	–	15	1
	Spring 08	107	–	–	5	5	–	10	–	–	–	–
	Summer 08	213	–	–	128	32	–	–	–	–	8	7
Big Spring stream	Fall 07	253	–	–	14	42	–	–	–	–	6	117
	Winter 08	206	–	–	36	8	–	–	–	–	14	92
	Spring 08	117	–	–	30	18	–	–	–	–	–	120
	Summer 08	61	–	–	109	44	–	–	–	–	2	54

In the Point-of-Rocks Spring system, Ash Meadows Amargosa pupfish capture was greatest in the upper 1,000 m. As with Kings Pool and Crystal Springs, Ash Meadows Amargosa pupfish was captured with greater frequency than crayfish, mosquitofish, or sailfin molly. Speckled dace was captured only in winter 2008 (n=5) and spring 2008 (n=2) in the Point-of-Rocks Spring system.

Bradford 1 and Bradford 2 Springs are relatively cool springs harboring Ash Meadows speckled dace and a few Ash Meadows Amargosa pupfish. Speckled dace capture was particularly high in Bradford 1 Spring ranging from 298 (summer 2008) to 771 (winter 2008) (table 3). Speckled dace was the predominant capture for all seasons except summer, when mosquitofish predominated. Crayfish captures were consistently the lowest for each season. No Ash Meadows Amargosa pupfish was found in Bradford 1 Spring but was found in Bradford 2 Spring (fig. 6).

In Forest Spring, seasonal Ash Meadows Amargosa pupfish captures ranged from 1 (fall 2007) to 55 (summer 2008) (fig. 6) and seasonal Ash Meadows speckled dace captures ranged from 1 (summer 2008) to 7 (winter 2008) (fig. 7). Mosquitofish was captured with the greatest frequency followed by crayfish (appendix C: table C1, figs. C1 and C5). Sailfin molly captures were low (appendix C: fig. C2).

During this study, no native fish were captured in Tubbs and Davis Springs. Davis Spring supported mosquitofish, black bullhead, and crayfish in fall 2007, winter 2008, and spring 2008. Davis Spring was chemically treated in 2008 with rotenone to eliminate black bullhead, and only crayfish were captured in summer 2008 (appendix C: table C1, figs. C1 and C5).

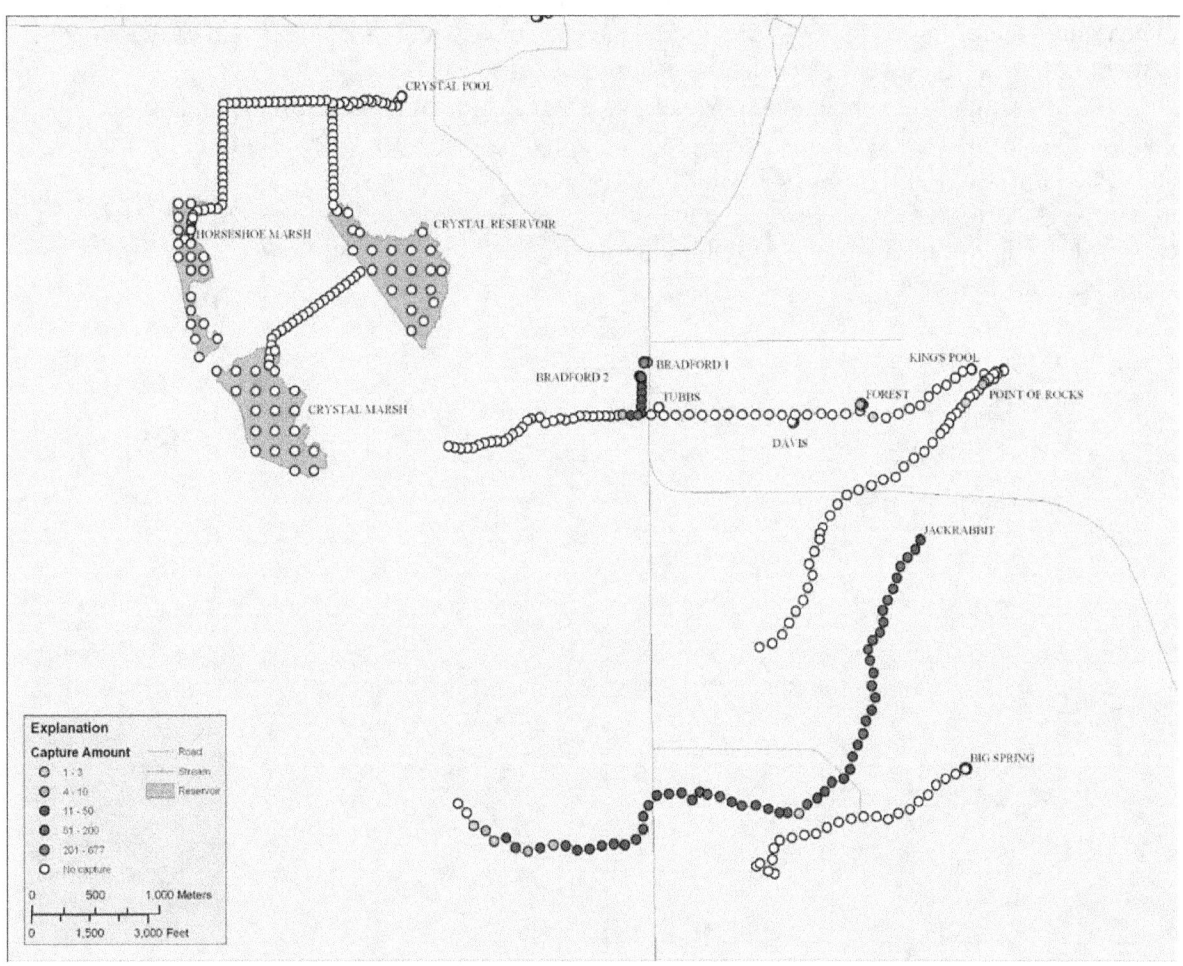

Figure 7. Relative abundance and distribution of Ash Meadows speckled dace in the southern springs, Ash Meadows National Wildlife Refuge, Nevada, fall 2007–summer 2008.

In Jackrabbit Spring, Ash Meadows Amargosa pupfish was the predominant species captured in the spring-pool with catches ranging from 786 (fall 2007) to 512 (summer 2008) although Ash Meadows speckled dace was the predominant species captured in the outflow with catches ranging from 659 (spring 2008) to 510 (fall 2007). During the four seasons of trapping in Jackrabbit Spring, speckled dace had been captured at every station except the lowest two (fig. 7). There were trends in Ash Meadows Amargosa pupfish and speckled dace seasonal outflow distribution that lend themselves well to kernel density estimation. The highest density of Ash Meadows Amargosa pupfish in Jackrabbit Spring outflow was in the upper 1,000 m, and particularly in the 500 m restoration site (fig. 8). About 8 percent of the total outflow supported 40–60 percent of the Ash Meadows Amargosa pupfish through the four seasons. Speckled dace also congregated at the restoration site especially in fall 2007 and winter 2008 with 33 percent of the captures there. In spring 2008, speckled dace was more widely dispersed and only about 14 percent of the captures were from the restoration area (fig. 9).

The capture frequency of Ash Meadows Amargosa pupfish was highest in Big Spring-pool in all seasons; however, few Ash Meadows Amargosa pupfish were found in the outflow and western mosquitofish was the predominant species. The greatest concentration of Ash Meadows Amargosa pupfish was in the upper 800 m of the stream. No speckled dace were captured in Big Spring. Crayfish was abundant in the outflow, but relatively few crayfish were captured from the spring-pool.

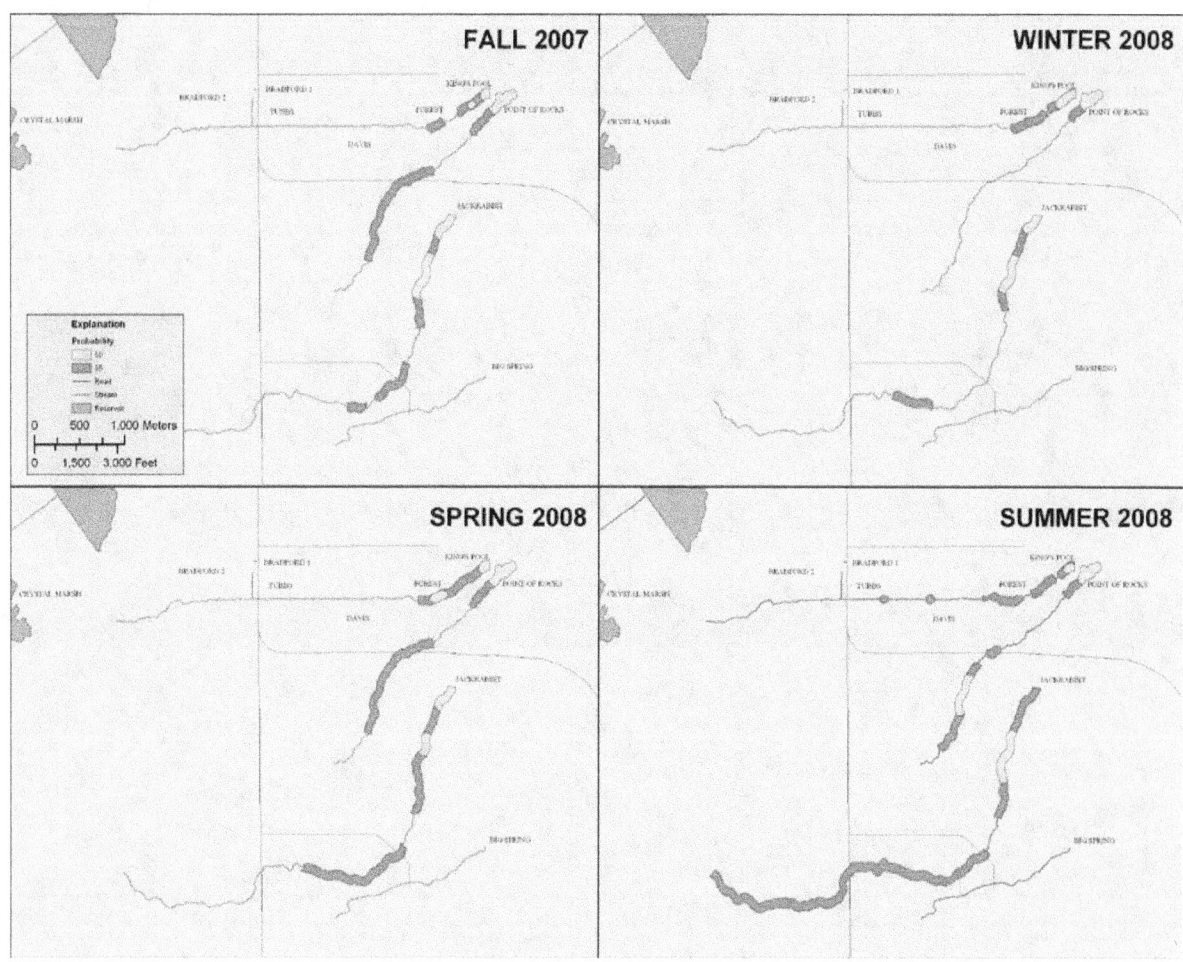

Figure 8. Kemel density estimations (50 and 95 percent probability) of Ash Meadows Amargosa pupfish in King's Pool, Point of Rocks, and Jackrabbit Springs, Ash Meadows National Wildlife Refuge, Nevada, fall 2007–summer 2008.

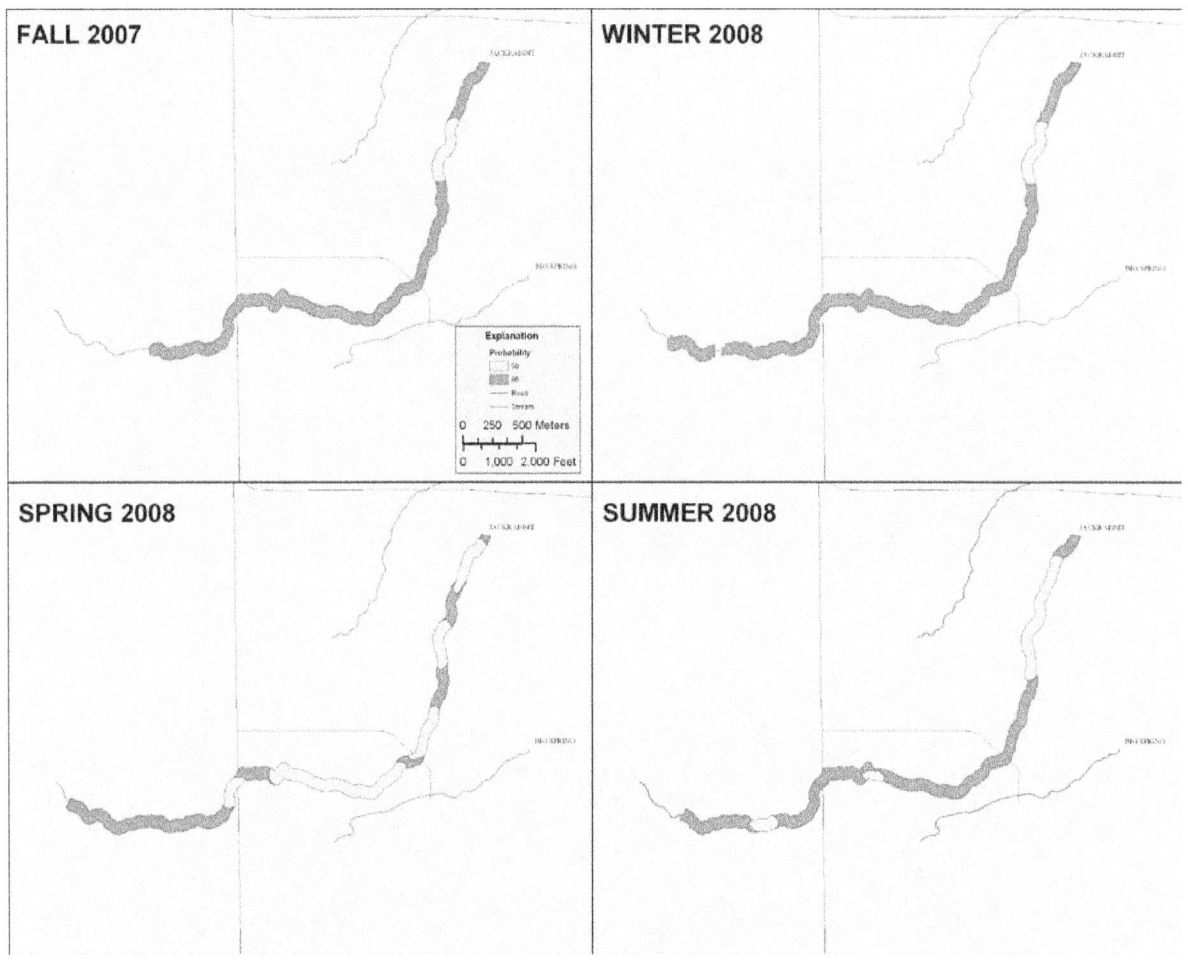

Figure 9. Kemel density estimations (50 and 95 percent probability) of Ash Meadows speckled dace in Jackrabbit Spring, Ash Meadows National Wildlife Refuge, Nevada, fall 2007–summer 2008.

Discussion

Although pupfish and speckled dace can survive and thrive in a wide variety of habitats (Moyle, 2002), there are habitat types that promote invasive species at the expense of pupfish and speckled dace (Scoppettone and others, 2005). The formation of Lower Crystal Marsh was an early Crystal Spring rehabilitation project to expand refuge wetlands and increase Ash Meadows Amargosa pupfish habitat (Threloff, 1991). The 42 ha wetland was completed in the early 1990s and within 2 years Ash Meadows Amargosa pupfish numbered more than 100,000 (Threloff, 1990). Thereafter, largemouth bass and green sunfish invaded the marsh, and our low Ash Meadows Amargosa pupfish captures suggest high predation. Lacustrine habitat not only serves as a haven for these predators, but can promote sailfin molly and mosquitofish as well. The formation of a headwater marsh immediately downstream of Kings Pool that was caused by a breach in a decaying and eroding outflow channel promoted sailfin molly, which was the predominant species there (Scoppettone and others, 2005). Formation of the Kings Pool headwater marsh began in 1989, and was capturing almost all the outflow water by 1994. In 1997, an outflow channel was excavated through the headwater marsh and trenched to an old irrigation ditch flowing west to into Forest and Bradford 2 Springs outflow. This restored reach transformed a sailfin molly-predominated marsh to an Ash Meadows Amargosa pupfish-predominated outflow. Our survey indicated that Ash Meadows Amargosa pupfish remained the predominant species in the outflow and in the spring-pool. Sailfin molly and mosquitofish were the predominant species in Kings Pool spring-pool prior to the restoration of the outflow, but Ash Meadows Amargosa pupfish predominated following restoration.

Native fish abundance in Bradford 1 and Bradford 2 Springs seem to be linked to status change of non-native species. Refuge personnel have been continually and systematically removing crayfish from Bradford 1 Spring, and these data suggest this measure has been effective. Seasonal numbers of Ash Meadows speckled dace reported from Bradford 1 Spring were much greater compared to an earlier estimate. In winter 2008, almost 700 individuals were captured, although in March 2002 only 63 ±4 were estimated (Leavy and others, 2004). Captures from Bradford 2 Spring were not as great as Bradford 1 Spring, but capture numbers and size structure suggest a reproductive population. In 1990, the Ash Meadows Amargosa pupfish population had been extirpated after a largemouth bass invasion. Bass has since been eliminated from the system and Ash Meadows Amargosa pupfish has been able to recolonize the spring after extensive crayfish removal (Leavy and others, 2004). One green sunfish was found in the system in 2001, and it was removed before substantial loss of Ash Meadows speckled dace (Leavy and others, 2004). Previous surveys of the Bradford Springs are difficult to compare with these results because the surveys were somewhat subjective (Hardy, 1979, Threloff, 1990) and report three Bradford springs while this study could only account for two springs. When those early surveys were conducted, Kings Pool outflow connected Bradford 1 and Bradford 2 Springs immediately adjacent to their respective spring-pools; whether this flow was perceived as a third spring is not clear.

Tubbs, Big, and Jackrabbit Springs reportedly harbored Ash Meadows speckled dace when the Ash Meadows NWR was established (Sada, 1990). The Tubbs Spring population of dace was estimated to be 35 fish, although no fish were captured by Threloff (1990) or during this study. In Big Spring, Ash Meadows speckled dace and Ash Meadows Amargosa pupfish were reported as common when the system was sampled in summer 1990 (Scoppettone and others, 1995), but by the late 1990s, the largemouth bass invasion into the spring became a persistent problem even after eradication efforts. At the end of this first year survey, largemouth bass were thought to be few or absent (Darrick Wessienfluh, Ash Meadows National Wildlife Refuge, oral commun., 2008). No Ash Meadows speckled dace were captured, suggesting that these fish were rare or have been extirpated from the Big Spring system. Ash Meadows Amargosa pupfish was common.

When the Ash Meadows NWR was established, Jackrabbit Spring was reported to harbor Ash Meadows speckled dace and Ash Meadows Amargosa pupfish (Williams and Sada, 1985) and it continues to do so. The Jackrabbit Spring fish community has not changed in more than 25 years. However, alterations made to the Jackrabbit environment, both floristic and hydraulic, would be expected to influence the abundance and distribution of native fishes. A fire along Jackrabbit outflow in August 2005 led to stream rehabilitation to protect the native species. Removal of tamarisk along the riparian corridor improved habitat conditions for native fishes (Kennedy and others, 2006). Marsh-like habitat along the course (which promotes nonnative fishes and crayfish) was transformed to a flowing stream, which was demonstrated to promote native fishes (Scoppettone and others, 2005). The most obvious change in native fish complement was a substantial increase in catch rate of speckled dace compared to the catch rate reported by Scoppettone and others (1995). The greatest concentration of native fishes in the stream was along the 500 m of restored habitat indicating, that at least in the early stage, the restoration was a success. Restoration habitat was transformed from marsh-like to flowing stream.

Forest and Point-of-Rocks Springs had relatively recent introductions of Ash Meadows speckled dace. Forest Spring was reported by Miller (1948) to have harbored Ash Meadows speckled dace, but Sada (1990) did not report Ash Meadows speckled dace when Ash Meadows NWR was established, and few Ash Meadows Amargosa pupfish were observed (Threloff, 1990). Forest Spring was one of several springs on the southern side of the Ash Meadows NWR to have been invaded by largemouth bass (chemically removed in 1998). We suspect that the few Ash Meadows Amargosa pupfish we captured from Forest Spring had re-colonized from Kings Pool Spring and the few Ash Meadows speckled dace captured were from those that had been introduced or had emigrated from Bradford 2 Spring.

The upper section of the Point-of-Rocks Spring system was restored in 2001 and converted from marsh-like to flowing stream. Although no baseline information on an Ash Meadows Amargosa pupfish population is available, we presume this restoration had a positive influence on Ash Meadows Amargosa pupfish. Outflow water temperature for these springs appeared suitable for Ash Meadows speckled dace, which were introduced in 2002 (Shawn Goodchild, U.S. Fish and Wildlife Service, oral commun.,2002). Few Ash Meadows speckled dace were captured, suggesting dace may be having difficulty establishing in a system with climax populations of crayfish and poeciliids.

Some changes have been made to aquatic habitats at the northern springs that would affect native fish communities, but not of the same magnitude as in the southern springs. The northern springs also have only one native fish species, Ash Meadows Amargosa pupfish. Of the northern springs, Fairbanks Spring probably has had the most fish community-altering changes since the establishment of the Ash Meadows NWR. Among the most outstanding changes were the 1998 fire along the course of the outflow, formation of headwater marsh, and the 2001 invasion of convict cichlids. The effect the fire had on the Ash Meadows Amargosa pupfish population is unknown, but formation of headwater marsh presumably had a negative effect (Scoppettone and others, 2005). Convict cichlids greatly suppressed the Ash Meadows Amargosa pupfish population. The planned restoration of Fairbanks Spring has the potential to positively influence the Ash Meadows Amargosa pupfish population.

Our captures of Ash Meadows Amargosa pupfish in the Rogers spring-pool were more than four times the estimates made in the early 1990s (Threloff, 1990; Scoppettone and others, 1995). No alteration to Rogers Spring has been documented and the reason for this increase is unknown.

The only change to Longstreet Spring has been directing the outflow to Petersen Reservoir intermittently since 1985, either through a pipe on its southwestern side of the spring-pool or an open ditch to the west. At the time of our survey, water was flowing down the open ditch and Ash Meadows Amargosa pupfish density in the outflow was among the lowest of the larger Ash Meadows springs. It is suspected that this low density is due, at least in part, to the greatly enlarged spring-pools that cool water from springs. Water temperature in the outflow is less than the Amargosa pupfish reproductive temperature minimum requirement of 26°C (Soltz and Naiman, 1978).

The primary impact to Warm Springs Amargosa pupfish habitat since the establishment of the Ash Meadows NWR has been the spread of crayfish and mosquitofish. When these two species first invaded the Warm Springs Complex is not clear, but these two species were not reported to be in Indian Spring in the early 1970s (Miller and Deacon, 1973). This is important because South Indian Spring is the first spring these species were documented to invade (Sada, 1990). Sometime after the early 1990s, crayfish and mosquitofish invaded North Indian Spring, and in the early 2000s, these fish were noted to have invaded School Springs, and more recently South Scruggs Spring. Warm Springs Amargosa pupfish no longer inhabit South Indian Spring and have a patchy distribution in South Scruggs Spring, which gives cause for concern that non-native species may continue to spread and cause a decline of Warm Springs Amargosa pupfish.

It has been previously demonstrated that non-native species have suppressed and replaced Ash Meadows' native fish populations (Scoppettone and others, 2005; Kennedy and others, 2006); this study adds further insight into the extent of non-native species impacts. For example, the Ash Meadows NWR chemical removal of non-native convict cichlid from Fairbanks Spring and mechanical removal of crayfish from Bradford 1 Spring were followed by substantial increases in native fish populations in those respective systems. Warm Springs Amargosa pupfish in North Indian Spring has been completely replaced by crayfish and mosquitofish. Additionally, Ash Meadows native fishes are now localized throughout their historical range, and non-natives species are presumably the cause.

Further data collection and analysis will be aimed at determining environmental factors that promote native fishes instead of crayfish, mosquitofish, and sailfin molly so that these environmental attributes can be integrated into restoration design and implementation. This study provides the baseline data for determining the success of future habitat design and modification.

Acknowledgments

Thanks to Ash Meadows National Wildlife Refuge for funding the project, and assisting us with lodging. Antonio Salgado (USGS), Mark Fabes (USGS), Sean Shea (USGS), Eric Miskow (Nevada Natural Heritage Program), and Shawn Goodchild (USFWS) assisted with fieldwork. Thanks to Tom Strekal (BIA Biologist, retired) for critical review.

References Cited

Baugh, T., Williams, J.E., Buck, D.A., and Deacon, J.E., 1986, New distributional records for *Cyprinodon nevadensis mionectes*, and endangered pupfish from Ash Meadows, Nevada: The Southwest Naturalist, v. 31, p. 544-546.

Deacon, J.E., Hubbs, C., and Zahuranec, B.J., 1964, Some effects of introduced fishes on the native fish fauna of southern Nevada: Copeia, p. 384-388.

Deacon, J.E., and Williams, C.D., 1991, Ash Meadows and the legacy of the Devils Hole pupfish, *in* Minckley, W.L., and Deacon, J.E. (eds.), Battle against extinction—Native fish management in the American West: Tucson, The University of Arizona Press, p. 69-87.

Dudley, W.W., Jr., and Larson, J.D., 1976, Effect of irrigation pumping on desert pupfish habitats in Ash Meadows, Nye County, Nevada: U.S. Geological Survey Professional Paper 927, 153 p.

Hardy, T., 1979, The inter-basin area report: Las Vegas, University of Nevada, U.S. Fish and Wild Service Agreement No. 14-16-001-6319-FS Amendment #4.

Hooge, P.N., and Eichenlaub, B., 1997, Animal movement extension to Arcview, ver. 1.1: Alaska Biological Science Center, U.S. Geological Survey, Anchorage, AK.

Hubbs, C., and Deacon, J.E., 1964, Additional introductions of tropical fishes into southern Nevada: Southwest Naturalist, v. 9, p. 249-251.

Gourley, C.R., and Ammon, E.M., 1997, Restoration of the Kings Spring drainage in Ash Meadows, Nevada: The Nature Conservancy of Nevada.

Kennedy, T.A., Finlay, J.C., and Hobbie, S.E., 2006, Eradication of invasive *Tamarix ramosissima* along a desert stream increase native fish density: Ecological Applications, v. 15, p. 2072-2083.

La Rivers, I., 1962, Fishes and fisheries of Nevada: Nevada State Fish and Game Commission, 782 p.

Leavy, T., McShane, R.R., Swaim, K.M., and Scoppettone G.G., 2004, Status of Ash Meadows speckled dace in Bradford Springs: Final report to the Las Vegas Office of the U.S. Fish and Wildlife Service, 12 p.

Miller, R.R., 1948, The cyprinodon fishes of Death Valley system of eastern California and southeastern Nevada: Miscellaneous Publications of the Museum of Zoology, University of Michigan, v. 529, 55 p.

Miller, R.R., and Deacon, J.E., 1973, New localities for the rare Warm Springs pupfish, *Cyprinodon nevadensis pectoralis*, from Ash Meadows, Nevada: Copeia, p. 137-140.

Moyle, P.B., 2002, Inland fishes of California: Berkeley, University of California Press.

Pister, E.P., 1974, Desert fishes and their habitats: Transactions of the American Fisheries Society, v. 103, p. 531-540.

Sada, D.W., 1990, Recovery plan for the endangered and threatened species of Ash Meadows, Nevada: Reno, Nev., U.S. Fish and Wildlife Service.

Scoppettone, G.G., Rissler, P.H., Byers, S., Shea, S., Nielsen, B., and Sjoberg, J., 1995, Information on the status and ecology of Ash Meadows Fishes and *Ambrysus*: National Biological Service, Reno Field Station, 111 p.

Scoppettone, G.G., Rissler, P.H., Gourley, C., and Martinez, C., 2005, Habitat restoration as a means of controlling non-native fish in a Mojave Desert Oasis: Restoration Ecology, v. 13, p. 247-256.

Soltz, K.L., and Naiman, R.J., 1978, The natural history of native fishes in the Death Valley system: Natural History Museum of Los Angeles County, California, Science Series, v. 30, 76 p.

Threloff, D., 1990, The distribution and abundance of the fishes of Ash Meadows—A preliminary inventory: Ash Meadow National Wildlife Refuge, U.S. Fish and Wildlife Service.

Threloff, D., 1991, Threatened And Endangered Species Use of a Restored Marsh on the Ash Meadows National Wildlife Refuge: Ash Meadow National Wildlife Refuge, U.S. Fish and Wildlife Service.

U.S. Department of the Interior, 1973, Threatened wildlife of the United States: U.S. Bureau of Sport Fisheries and Wildlife Resources Publication 114, 289 p.

U.S. Environmental Protection Agency, 2010, National Environmental Policy Act (NEPA).

Williams, B.K., Nichols, J.D., and Conroy, M.J., 2001, Analysis and management of animal populations (modeling, estimation, and decision making): San Francisco, Calif., Academic Press.

Williams, J.E., and Deacon, J.E., 1986, Sub-specific identity of the Amargosa pupfish, *Cyprinodon nevadensis*, from Crystal Spring, Ash Meadows, Nevada: Great Basin Naturalist, v. 46, p. 220-223.

Williams, J.E., and Sada, D.W., 1985, Status of two endangered fishes, *Cyprinodon nevadensis mionectes* and *Rhinichthys osculus nevadensis,* from two springs in Ash Meadows, Nevada: Southwestern Naturalist, v. 30, p. 475-484.

Worton, B.J., 1987, A review of models of home range for animal movement: Ecological Modeling, v. 38, p. 277-298.

Appendix A. Seasonal Distributions of Fishes and Crayfish at Ash Meadows National Wildlife Refuge, Nevada

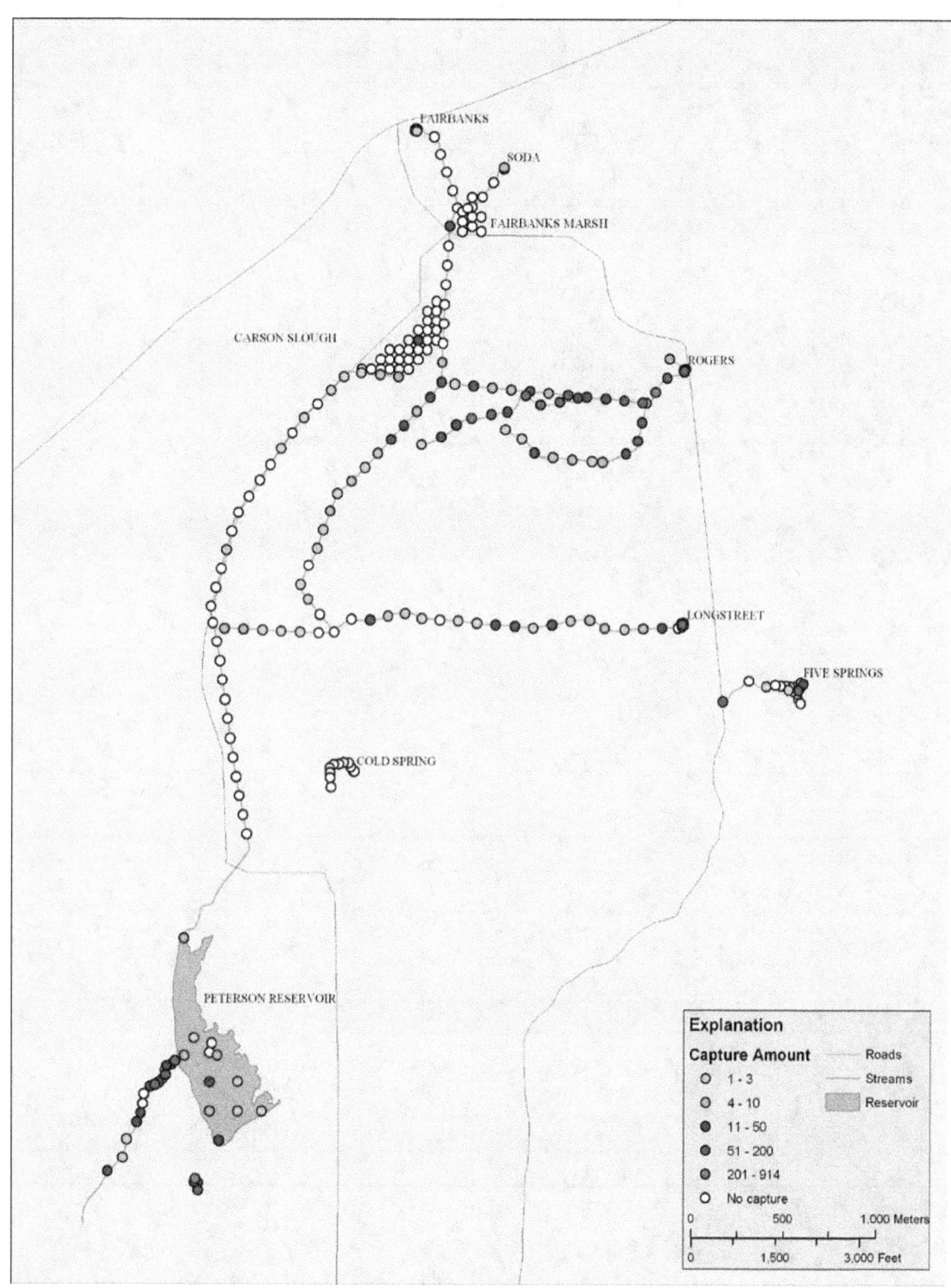

Figure A1. Composite relative abundance and seasonal distribution of mosquitofish in the northern springs, Ash Meadows National Wildlife Refuge, Nevada, fall 2007–summer 2008.

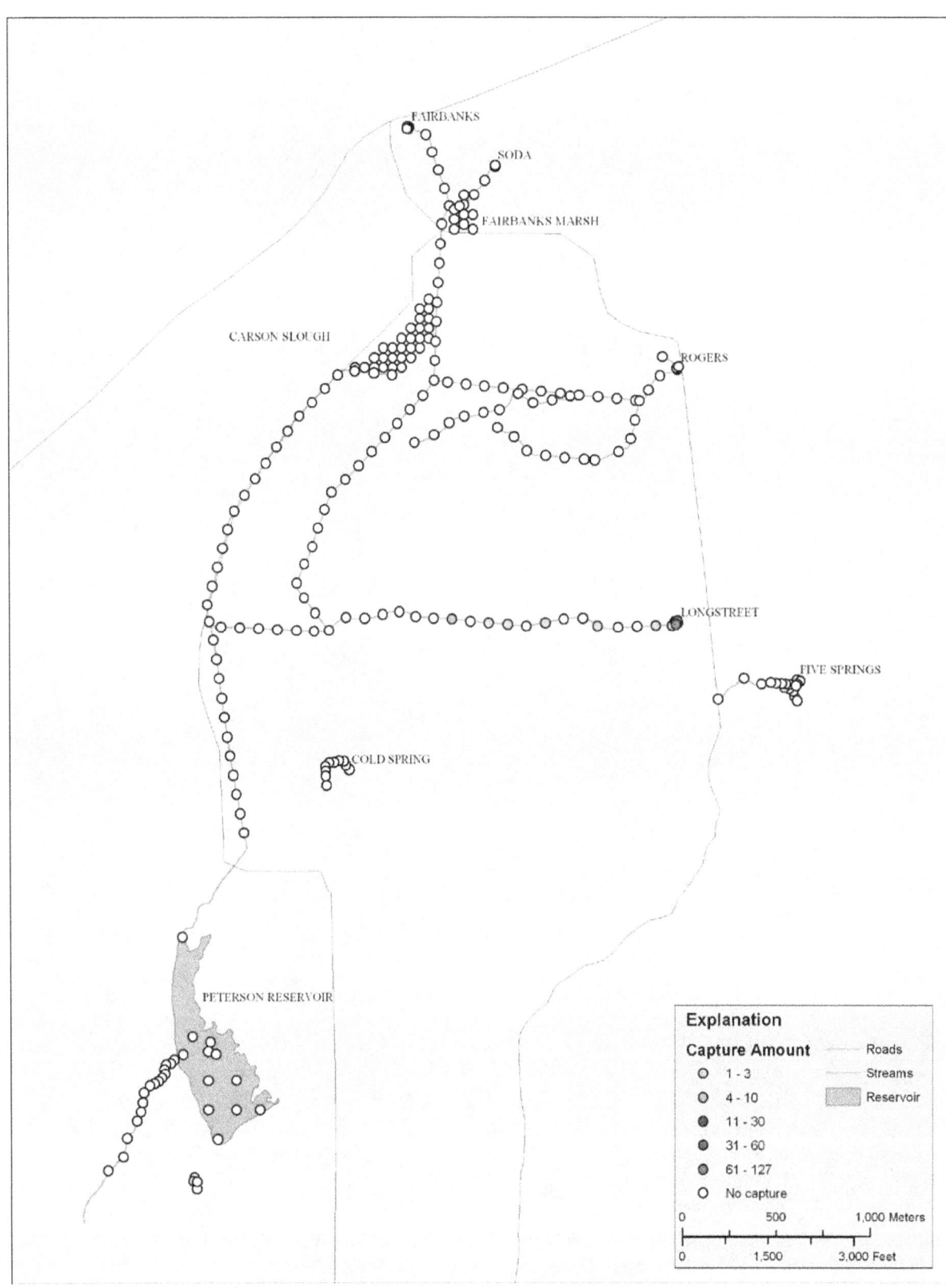

Figure A2. Composite relative abundance and seasonal distribution of sailfin mollies in the northern springs, Ash Meadows National Wildlife Refuge, Nevada, fall 2007–summer 2008.

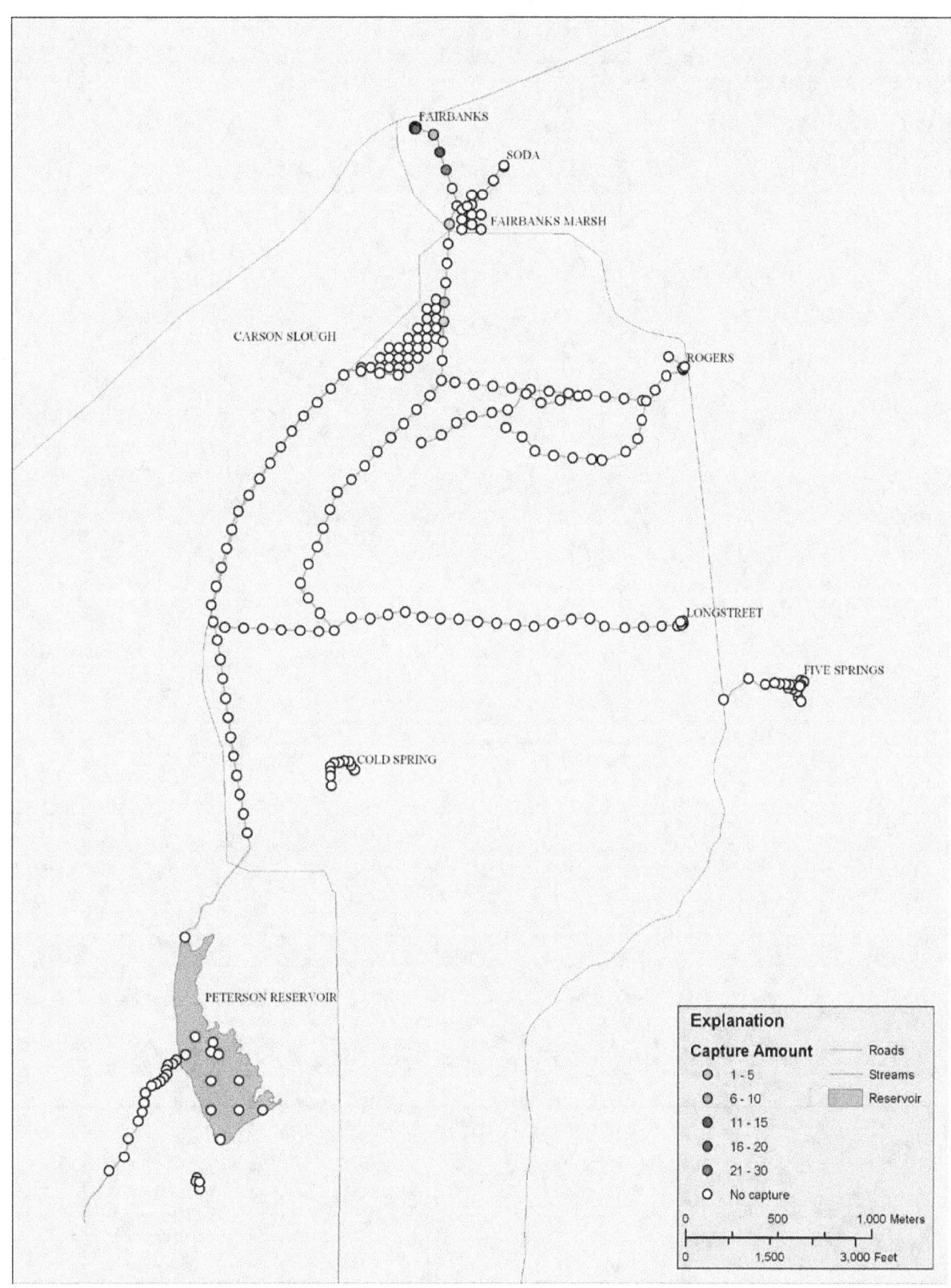

Figure A3. Composite relative abundance and seasonal distribution of convict cichlids in the northern springs, Ash Meadows National Wildlife Refuge, Nevada, fall 2007–summer 2008.

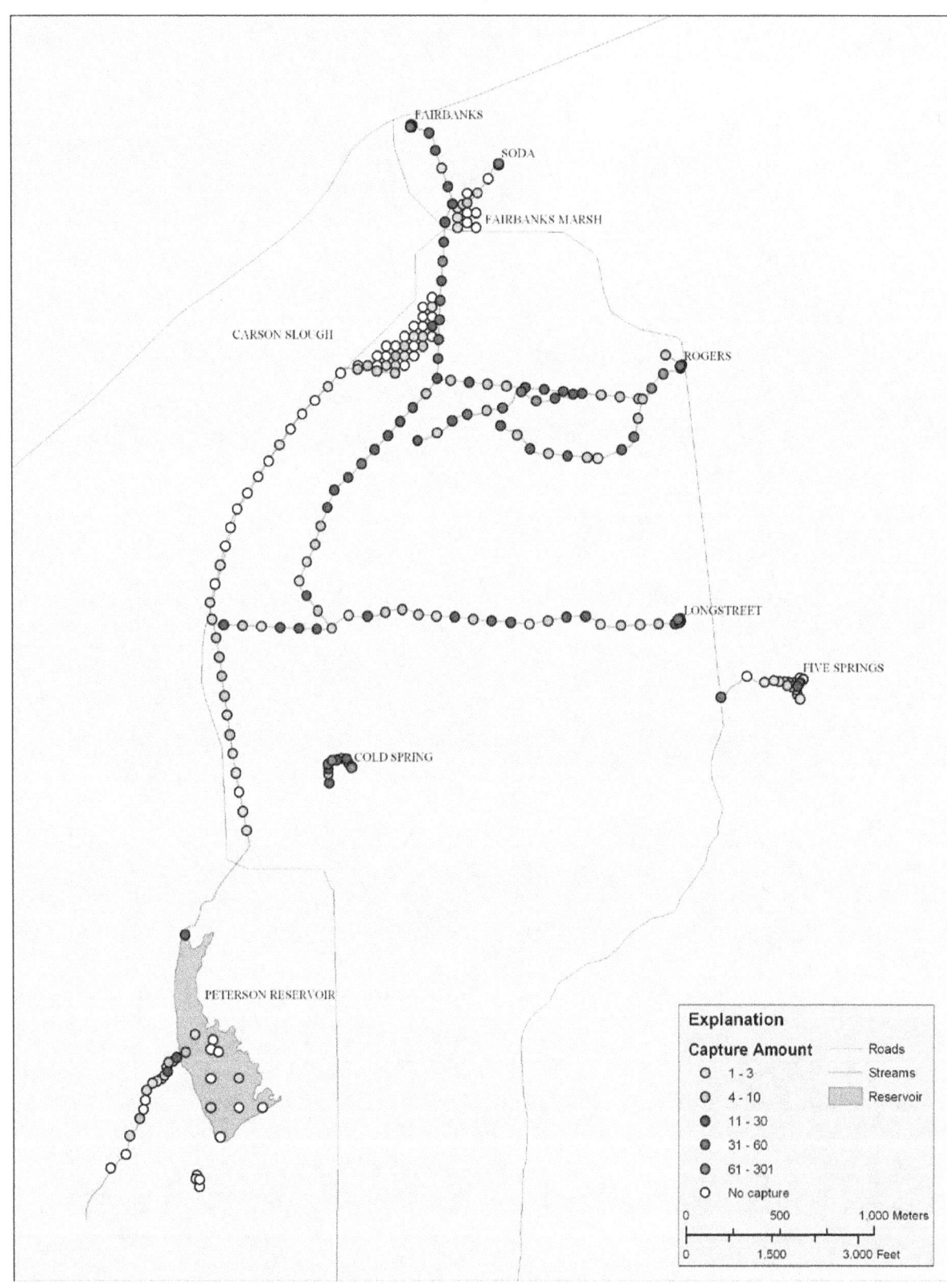

Figure A4. Composite relative abundance and seasonal distribution of crayfish in the northern springs, Ash Meadows National Wildlife Refuge, Nevada, fall 2007–summer 20

Table A1. Species, number, efficiency, and size captured seasonally at the northern springs systems of the Ash Meadows National Wildlife Refuge, Nevada, fall 2007–summer 2008.

[Spring locations are shown in figures 1 and 2. FL, fork length. Species: CYMI, Ash Meadows Amargosa pupfish; CYPE, Warm Springs Amargosa pupfish; RHON, Ash Meadows speckled dace; GAAF, Mosquitofish; POLA, Sailfin Molly; LECY, Green Sunfish; MISA, Largemouth Bass; ARNI, Convict Cichlid; AMME, Black Bullhead; LICA, Bull Frog; PRCL, Red Swamp Crayfish]

Fall 2007

System	Species	Total catch	Average/trap	n	FL (min-max)	Average ±Standard Deviation
Fairbanks Spring-pool	CYMI	453	75.5	117	25–47	35 ±5
	GAAF	1	0.2	1	37	37
	ARNI	50	8.3	50	28–62	43 ±8
	LICA	5	0.8	5	45–65	57 ±8
	PRCL	4	0.7	4	54–65	59 ±6
Fairbanks stream	CYMI	457	6.9	175	17–54	34 ±7
	GAAF	200	3.0	101	20–54	35 ±8
	ARNI	72	1.1	40	25–65	50 ±9
	LICA	4	0.1	–	–	–
	PRCL	144	2.2	144	17–72	53 ±12
Fairbanks marsh	PRCL	2	0.3	2	64–68	66 ±3
Carson Slough marsh	CYMI	4	0.4	4	27–35	30 ±4
	GAAF	11	1.0	10	22–42	31 ±6
	PRCL	50	4.5	48	21–72	48 ±15
Soda spring-pool	GAAF	8	8.0	8	21–31	26 ±3
	PRCL	12	12.0	12	30–64	46 ±12
Soda stream	GAAF	3	1.0	3	20–28	24 ±4
	PRCL	12	4.0	12	22–64	46 ±12
Rogers spring-pool	CYMI	410	68.3	100	18–42	28 ±5
	GAAF	42	7.0	42	18–43	25 ±5
	LICA	12	2.0	12	10–64	43 ±16
	PRCL	12	2.0	12	34–53	45 ±6
Rogers stream	CYMI	44	1.3	39	15–41	30 ±6
	GAAF	485	13.9	182	20–49	31 ±7
	LICA	1	–	1	42	42
	PRCL	214	6.1	160	20–75	49 ±13
Longstreet spring-pool	CYMI	546	91.0	50	20–50	30 ±8
	GAAF	56	9.3	24	22–44	29 ±6
	POLA	53	8.8	43	16–58	34 ±10
	PRCL	17	2.8	17	33–75	51 ±11
Longstreet stream	CYMI	3	0.2	3	32–40	36 ±4
	GAAF	7	0.4	7	26–43	35 ±6
	POLA	2	0.1	2	28–33	31 ±4
	PRCL	33	1.8	31	26–72	51 ±12
Five Springs spring-pool	CYMI	32	6.4	11	18–36	30 ±5
	GAAF	–	–	–	–	–
	PRCL	2	0.4	2	50–51	51 ±1
Five Springs stream	CYMI	4	0.3	4	23–25	25 ±1
	GAAF	13	0.9	13	21–54	33 ±12
	PRCL	7	0.5	7	32–63	51 ±12
Peterson Reservoir	CYMI	44	4.0	41	17–33	24 ±4
	GAAF	2	0.2	2	23–36	30 ±9
	PRCL	3	0.3	3	28–56	41 ±14
Peterson stream	CYMI	351	17.6	79	14–52	28 ±6
	GAAF	75	3.8	43	18–47	30 ±7
	PRCL	1	0.1	1	24	24
Cold spring-pool	PRCL	17	17.0	17	14–70	50 ±15
Cold stream	CYMI	3	0.3	3	26–46	37 ±10
	PRCL	39	3.9	35	19–74	52 ±15
Cold pool	PRCL	25	25.0	10	23–68	46 ±13

Table A1. Species, number, efficiency, and size captured seasonally at the northern springs systems of the Ash Meadows National Wildlife Refuge, Nevada, fall 2007–summer 2008.—Continued

Winter 2008

System	Species	Total catch	Average/trap	n	FL (min-max)	Average ±Standard Deviation
Fairbanks Spring-pool	CYMI	581	96.8	86	24–45	34 ±5
	GAAF	–	–	–	–	–
	ARNI	–	–	–	–	–
	LICA	–	–	–	–	–
	PRCL	18	3.0	18	22–61	36 ±12
Fairbanks stream	CYMI	149	3.1	40	25–45	34 ±5
	GAAF	–	–	–	–	–
	ARNI	–	–	–	–	–
	LICA	–	–	–	–	–
	PRCL	131	2.7	127	21–74	52 ±12
Fairbanks marsh	PRCL	–	–	–	–	–
Carson Slough marsh	CYMI	–	–	–	–	–
	GAAF	–	–	–	–	–
	PRCL	–	–	–	–	–
Soda spring-pool	GAAF	–	–	–	–	–
	PRCL	18	18.0	18	31–61	47 ±10
Soda stream	GAAF	–	–	–	–	–
	PRCL	5	1.7	5	41–65	56 ±9
Rogers spring-pool	CYMI	466	77.7	103	15–40	26 ±4
	GAAF	69	11.5	42	19–39	27 ±5
	LICA	29	4.8	0	–	–
	PRCL	27	4.5	27	22–55	41 ±7
Rogers stream	CYMI	59	1.6	58	19–52	31 ±6
	GAAF	123	3.3	66	21–44	29 ±5
	LICA	1	–	1	115	115
	PRCL	227	6.1	176	23–75	50 ±11
Longstreet spring-pool	CYMI	332	55.3	100	17–48	31 ±7
	GAAF	36	6.0	36	21–45	30 ±7
	POLA	19	3.2	19	24–54	39 ±9
	PRCL	23	3.8	23	31–72	49 ±12
Longstreet stream	CYMI	22	1.2	22	20–45	35 ±6
	GAAF	6	0.3	6	25–38	32 ±5
	POLA	1	0.1	1	52	52
	PRCL	22	1.2	22	29–64	47 ±11
Five Springs spring-pool	CYMI	21	5.3	21	20–34	26 ±4
	GAAF	9	2.3	9	20–34	29 ±4
	PRCL	1	0.3	1	62	62
Five Springs stream	CYMI	3	0.3	3	25–40	33 ±8
	GAAF	57	5.2	19	23–60	33 ±10
	PRCL	20	1.8	18	28–65	48 ±11
Peterson reservoir	CYMI	2	0.2	2	22–24	23 ±1
	GAAF	–	–	–	–	–
	PRCL	1	0.1	1	26	26
Peterson stream	CYMI	108	10.8	44	15–43	26 ±6
	GAAF	5	0.5	5	25–47	34 ±9
	PRCL	28	2.8	25	20–65	33 ±10
Cold spring-pool	PRCL	45	45.0	20	27–71	40 ±13
Cold stream	CYMI	–	–	–	–	–
	PRCL	113	11.3	74	20–68	49 ±12
Cold pool	PRCL	32	32.0	10	31–68	47 ±12

Table A1. Species, number, efficiency, and size captured seasonally at the northern springs systems of the Ash Meadows National Wildlife Refuge, Nevada, fall 2007–summer 2008.—Continued

Spring 2008

System	Species	Total catch	Average/trap	n	FL (min-max)	Average ±Standard Deviation
Fairbanks Spring-pool	CYMI	358	59.7	126	18–57	34 ±7
	GAAF	–	–	–	–	–
	ARNI	–	–	–	–	–
	LICA	–	–	–	–	–
	PRCL	21	3.5	21	27–69	50 ±10
Fairbanks stream	CYMI	284	5.8	135	11–52	30 ±9
	GAAF	2	–	2	27–47	37 ±14
	ARNI	–	–	–	–	–
	LICA	7	0.1	0	–	–
	PRCL	196	4.0	179	21–78	49 ±12
Fairbanks marsh	PRCL	6	0.8	6	32–69	47 ±15
Carson Slough marsh	CYMI	–	–	–	–	–
	GAAF	–	–	–	–	–
	PRCL	–	–	–	–	–
Soda spring-pool	GAAF	–	–	–	–	–
	PRCL	13	13.0	10	41–62	52 ±7
Soda stream	GAAF	–	–	–	–	–
	PRCL	8	2.7	8	32–65	50 ±10
Rogers spring-pool	CYMI	340	56.7	88	17–40	27 ±5
	GAAF	39	6.5	20	19–34	24 ±3
	LICA	9	1.5	0	–	–
	PRCL	31	5.2	31	29–57	43 ±7
Rogers stream	CYMI	149	4.0	70	21–46	32 ±6
	GAAF	250	6.8	151	20–47	32 ±6
	LICA	2	0.1	2	91–92	92 ±1
	PRCL	184	5.0	147	21–74	51 ±11
Longstreet spring-pool	CYMI	353	58.8	101	18–53	33 ±7
	GAAF	1	0.2	1	31	31
	POLA	45	7.5	38	20–52	34 ±8
	PRCL	23	3.8	23	37–67	51 ±9
Longstreet stream	CYMI	95	5.0	66	20–57	36 ±7
	GAAF	39	2.1	36	21–47	33 ±7
	POLA	5	0.3	5	20–50	33 ±12
	PRCL	53	2.8	53	27–70	51 ±11
Five Springs spring-pool	CYMI	23	4.6	23	22–33	26 ±3
	GAAF	5	1.0	5	23–31	26 ±3
	PRCL	5	1.0	5	47–51	49 ±2
Five Springs stream	CYMI	13	1.0	13	22–33	27 ±4
	GAAF	75	5.8	21	22–52	29 ±9
	PRCL	9	0.7	9	20–68	44 ±18
Peterson reservoir	CYMI	12	1.1	12	20–33	27 ±4
	GAAF	–	–	–	–	–
	PRCL	4	0.4	4	46–75	57 ±13
Peterson stream	CYMI	861	43.1	172	19–43	31 ±5
	GAAF	11	0.6	10	27–62	38 ±10
	PRCL	8	0.4	8	42–83	52 ±13
Cold spring-pool	PRCL	32	32.0	9	33–67	50 ±13
Cold stream	CYMI	4	0.5	4	28–37	33 ±4
	PRCL	54	6.8	44	27–67	49 ±9
Cold pool	PRCL	18	18.0	10	23–67	45 ±11

Table A1. Species, number, efficiency, and size captured seasonally at the northern springs systems of the Ash Meadows National Wildlife Refuge, Nevada, fall 2007–summer 2008.—Continued

			Summer 2008			
System	Species	Total catch	Average/trap	n	FL (min-max)	Average ±Standard Deviation
Fairbanks Spring-pool	CYMI	821	136.8	133	17–55	32 ±6
	GAAF	–	–	–	–	–
	ARNI	–	–	–	–	–
	LICA	–	–	–	–	–
	PRCL	35	5.8	15	42–73	63 ±8
Fairbanks stream	CYMI	2,235	45.6	341	18–50	31 ±6
	GAAF	45	0.9	38	21–45	31 ±7
	ARNI	–	–	–	–	–
	LICA	–	–	–	–	–
	PRCL	295	6.0	165	24–73	52 ±11
Fairbanks marsh	PRCL	–	–	–	–	–
Carson Slough marsh	CYMI	–	–	–	–	–
	GAAF	–	–	–	–	–
	PRCL	–	–	–	–	–
Soda spring-pool	GAAF	–	–	–	–	–
	PRCL	16	16.0	16	30–64	49 ±10
Soda stream	GAAF	–	–	–	–	–
	PRCL	3	1.5	3	27–60	48 ±19
Rogers spring-pool	CYMI	341	56.8	125	19–41	28 ±4
	GAAF	248	41.3	95	15–36	26 ±6
	LICA	2	0.3	0	–	–
	PRCL	32	5.3	31	30–65	45 ±9
Rogers stream	CYMI	60	1.8	60	15–46	31 ±6
	GAAF	919	27.8	230	19–47	33 ±6
	LICA	–	–	–	–	–
	PRCL	144	4.4	114	20–72	52 ±11
Longstreet spring-pool	CYMI	458	76.3	132	16–52	29 ±7
	GAAF	80	13.3	72	18–50	28 ±7
	POLA	133	22.2	112	16–52	33 ±8
	PRCL	69	11.5	62	15–69	44 ±11
Longstreet stream	CYMI	98	5.4	87	16–45	27 ±8
	GAAF	73	4.1	62	21–45	33 ±7
	POLA	4	0.2	4	25–50	37 ±11
	PRCL	68	3.8	62	22–72	52 ±11
Five Springs spring-pool	CYMI	21	4.2	21	15–36	26 ±6
	GAAF	3	0.6	3	23–27	25 ±2
	PRCL	–	–	–	–	–
Five Springs stream	CYMI	46	3.3	12	23–38	31 ±5
	GAAF	68	4.9	22	18–50	29 ±7
	PRCL	41	2.9	28	24–70	52 ±13
Peterson reservoir	CYMI	157	14.3	60	13–41	23 ±7
	GAAF	95	8.6	41	18–40	26 ±6
	PRCL	3	0.3	3	48–73	63 ±13
Peterson stream	CYMI	514	27.1	137	17–43	29 ±5
	GAAF	1164	61.3	150	15–62	34 ±9
	PRCL	20	1.1	19	43–73	65 ±8
Cold spring-pool	PRCL	33	33.0	10	38–70	56 ±11
Cold stream	CYMI	–	–	–	–	–
	PRCL	68	8.5	59	12–70	52 ±11
Cold pool	PRCL	16	16.0	10	36–61	49 ±8

Appendix B. Seasonal Distributions of Fishes and Crayfish at Warm Springs Complex, Ash Meadows National Wildlife Refuge, Nevada

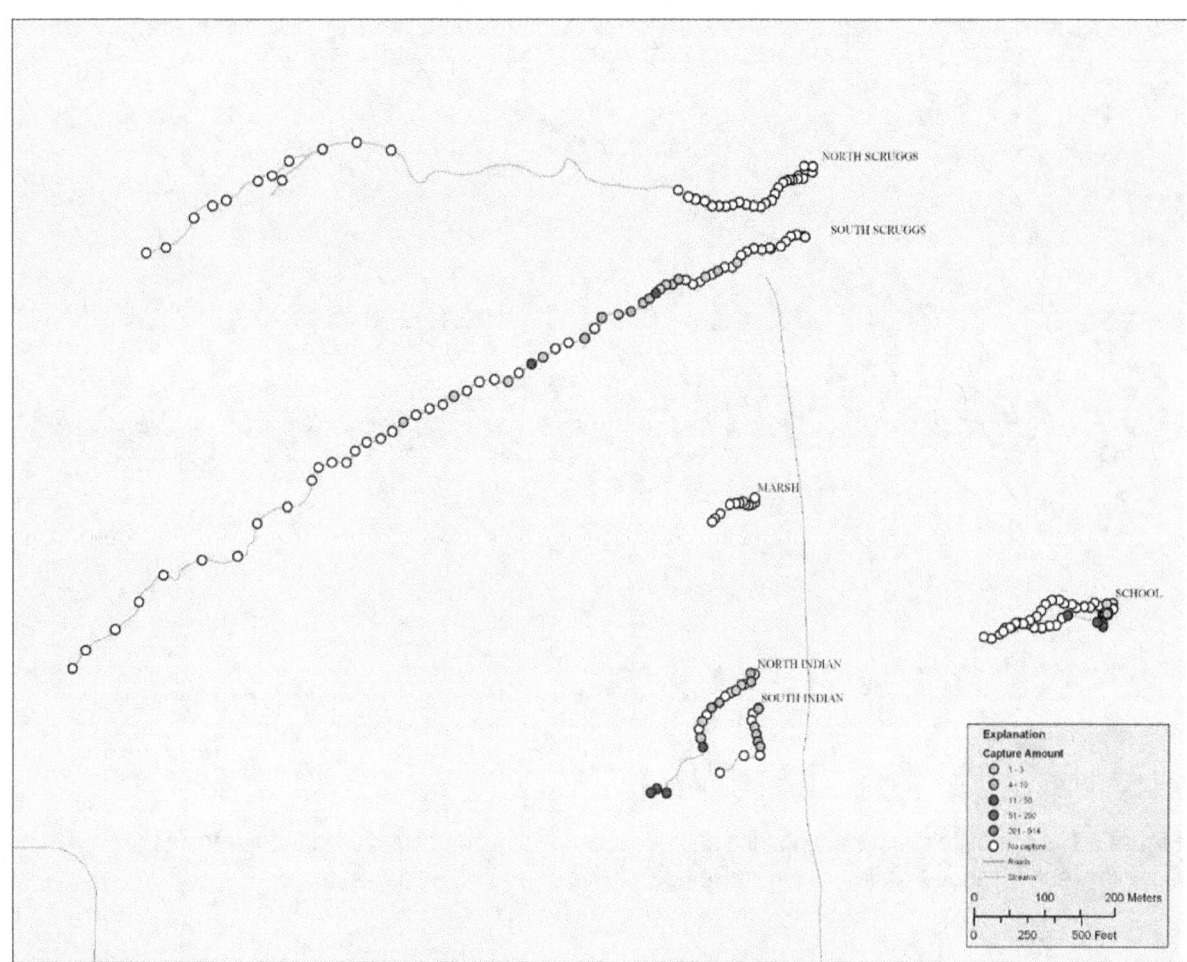

Figure B1. Composite relative abundance and seasonal distribution of mosquitofish in the Warm Springs Complex, Ash Meadows National Wildlife Refuge, Nevada, fall 2007–summer 2008.

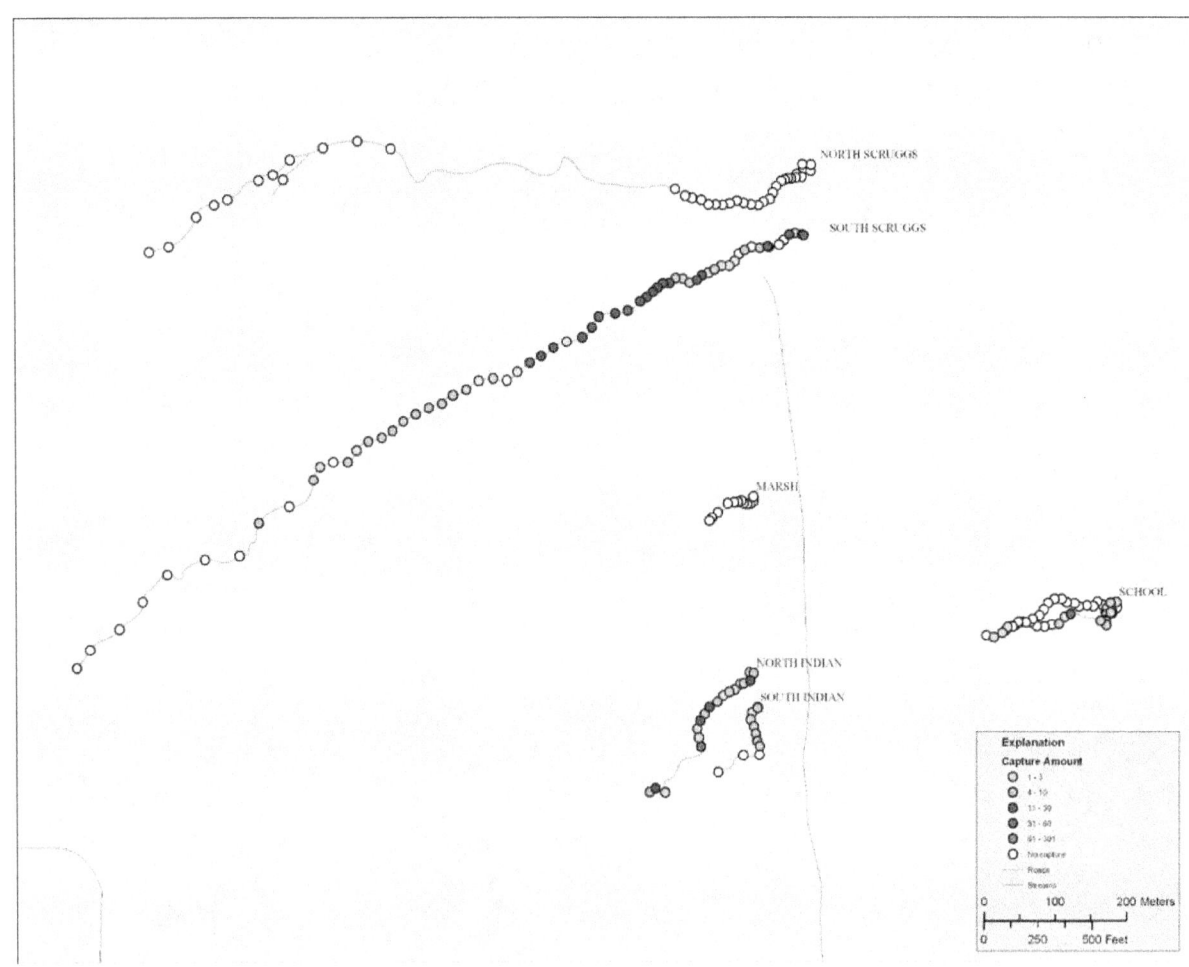

Figure B2. Composite relative abundance and seasonal distribution of crayfish in the Warm Springs Complex, Ash Meadows National Wildlife Refuge, Nevada, fall 2007–summer 2008.

Table B1. Species, number, efficiency, and size captured seasonally at the Warm Springs Complex of the Ash Meadows National Wildlife Refuge, Nevada, fall 2007–summer 2008.

[Spring locations are shown in figures 1 and 2. FL, fork length. Species: CYMI, Ash Meadows Amargosa pupfish; CYPE, Warm Springs Amargosa pupfish; RHON, Ash Meadows speckled dace; GAAF, Mosquitofish; POLA, Sailfin Molly; LECY, Green Sunfish; MISA, Largemouth Bass; ARNI, Convict Cichlid; AMME, Black Bullhead; LICA, Bull Frog; PRCL, Red Swamp Crayfish]

			Fall 2007			
System	Species	Total catch	Average/trap	n	FL (min-max)	Average ±Standard Deviation
North Scruggs spring-pool	CYPE	–	–	–	–	–
North Scruggs stream	CYPE	86	3.4	85	13–41	28 ±6
South Scruggs spring-pool	CYPE	17	17.0	17	17–27	21 ±3
	PRCL	6	6.0	6	34–66	47 ±11
South Scruggs stream	CYPE	40	0.7	40	12–48	28 ±10
	GAAF	16	0.3	16	12–42	30 ±8
	PRCL	157	2.9	157	10–81	46 ±12
Marsh spring-pool	CYPE	–	–	–	–	–
Marsh stream	CYPE	168	14.0	72	22–44	31 ±5
North Indian spring-pool	CYPE	–	–	–	–	–
	PRCL	3	3.0	3	16–60	36 ±22
North Indian stream	CYPE	79	4.4	37	17–45	29 ±7
	GAAF	62	3.4	47	19–48	30 ±6
	LICA	–	–	–	–	–
	PRCL	55	3.1	48	17–68	44 ±14
South Indian stream	GAAF	22	3.1	22	21–42	28 ±5
	PRCL	15	2.1	15	27–66	50 ±11
School spring-pool	CYPE	19	9.5	19	17–30	23 ±4
	GAAF	3	1.5	3	18–27	23 ±5
	PRCL	4	2.0	4	45–59	55 ±6
School ponds	CYPE	294	32.7	92	17–41	27 ±6
	GAAF	50	5.6	38	21–55	32 ±8
	PRCL	21	2.3	21	32–70	51 ±11
School stream	CYPE	62	3.9	62	15–45	25 ±6
	GAAF	40	2.5	18	23–38	28 ±5
	PRCL	41	2.6	31	13–72	47 ±17

Table B1. Species, number, efficiency, and size captured seasonally at the Warm Springs Complex of the Ash Meadows National Wildlife Refuge, Nevada.—Continued

Winter 2008

System	Species	Total catch	Average/trap	n	FL (min-max)	Average ±Standard Deviation
North Scruggs spring-pool	CYPE	–	–	–	–	–
North Scruggs stream	CYPE	84	2.8	71	15–45	32 ±7
South Scruggs spring-pool	CYPE	–	–	–	–	–
	PRCL	1	1.0	1	43	43
South Scruggs stream	CYPE	57	1.0	57	14–46	28 ±9
	GAAF	14	0.3	14	18–40	29 ±6
	PRCL	131	2.3	112	18–68	44 ±11
Marsh spring-pool	CYPE	–	–	–	–	–
Marsh stream	CYPE	171	14.3	72	20–46	32 ±6
North Indian spring-pool	CYPE	1	1.0	1	29	29
	PRCL	4	4.0	4	32–68	44 ±16
North Indian stream	CYPE	34	2.0	23	19–43	28 ±7
	GAAF	17	1.0	17	21–36	28 ±4
	LICA	2	0.1	2	50–51	51 ±1
	PRCL	34	2.0	31	21–61	42 ±10
South Indian stream	GAAF	2	0.3	2	35–37	36 ±1
	PRCL	9	1.1	9	25–59	44 ±11
School spring-pool	CYPE	4	2.0	4	18–22	20 ±2
	GAAF	–	–	–	–	–
	PRCL	–	–	–	–	–
School ponds	CYPE	267	44.5	120	16–42	26 ±6
	GAAF	45	7.5	40	20–55	31 ±8
	PRCL	3	0.5	2	65	65
School stream	CYPE	116	11.6	80	18–44	25 ±6
	GAAF	24	2.4	22	21–41	27 ±8
	PRCL	43	4.3	14	31–72	42 ±10

Table B1. Species, number, efficiency, and size captured seasonally at the Warm Springs Complex of the Ash Meadows National Wildlife Refuge, Nevada.—Continued

Spring 2008

System	Species	Total catch	Average/trap	n	FL (min-max)	Average ±Standard Deviation
North Scruggs spring-pool	CYPE	7	3.5	7	21–38	26 ±6
North Scruggs stream	CYPE	81	3.0	81	17–48	29 ±8
South Scruggs spring-pool	CYPE	4	4.0	4	22–24	23 ±1
	PRCL	4	4.0	4	50–58	56 ±4
South Scruggs stream	CYPE	52	0.9	51	16–49	26 ±8
	GAAF	37	0.7	29	20–52	31 ±9
	PRCL	119	2.2	119	22–65	45 ±12
Marsh spring-pool	CYPE	1	1.0	1	38	38
Marsh stream	CYPE	141	11.8	64	18–46	31 ±7
North Indian spring-pool	CYPE	1	1.0	1	30	30
	PRCL	–	–	–	–	–
North Indian stream	CYPE	35	2.1	14	18–35	29 ±5
	GAAF	15	0.9	15	21–48	32 ±7
	LICA	–	–	–	–	–
	PRCL	28	1.6	27	27–61	44 ±10
South Indian stream	GAAF	3	0.4	3	22–35	27 ±7
	PRCL	4	0.6	4	42–58	49 ±7
School spring-pool	CYPE	–	–	–	–	–
	GAAF	–	–	–	–	–
	PRCL	–	–	–	–	–
School ponds	CYPE	–	–	–	–	–
	GAAF	–	–	–	–	–
	PRCL	–	–	–	–	–
School stream	CYPE	–	–	–	–	–
	GAAF	–	–	–	–	–
	PRCL	–	–	–	–	–

Table B1. Species, number, efficiency, and size captured seasonally at the Warm Springs Complex of the Ash Meadows National Wildlife Refuge, Nevada.—Continued

Summer 2008

System	Species	Total catch	Average/trap	n	FL (min-max)	Average ±Standard Deviation
North Scruggs spring-pool	CYPE	16	8.0	16	18–35	26 ±5
North Scruggs stream	CYPE	115	5.5	115	17–45	26 ±7
South Scruggs spring-pool	CYPE	2	2.0	2	18–21	20 ±2
	PRCL	9	9.0	9	37–68	55 ±9
South Scruggs stream	CYPE	51	0.9	33	17–47	31 ±9
	GAAF	21	0.4	20	19–38	29 ±6
	PRCL	103	1.9	102	15–64	45 ±11
Marsh spring-pool	CYPE	–	–	–	–	–
Marsh stream	CYPE	152	12.7	82	17–50	32 ±6
North Indian spring-pool	CYPE	1	1.0	1	33	33
	PRCL	3	3.0	3	47–52	50 ±3
North Indian stream	CYPE	32	2.1	16	26–39	33 ±4
	GAAF	4	0.3	4	28–37	32 ±4
	LICA	–	–	–	–	–
	PRCL	23	1.5	22	24–53	38 ±8
South Indian stream	GAAF	3	0.4	3	32–37	34 ±3
	PRCL	5	0.6	5	47–64	57 ±7
School spring-pool	CYPE	6	3.0	6	23–29	26 ±2
	GAAF	–	–	–	–	–
	PRCL	–	–	–	–	–
School ponds	CYPE	–	–	–	–	–
	GAAF	–	–	–	–	–
	PRCL	–	–	–	–	–
School stream	CYPE	177	16.1	70	16–46	29 ±6
	GAAF	–	–	–	–	–
	PRCL	–	–	–	–	–

Appendix C. Seasonal Distributions of Fishes and Crayfish in Southern Springs, Ash Meadows National Wildlife Refuge, Nevada

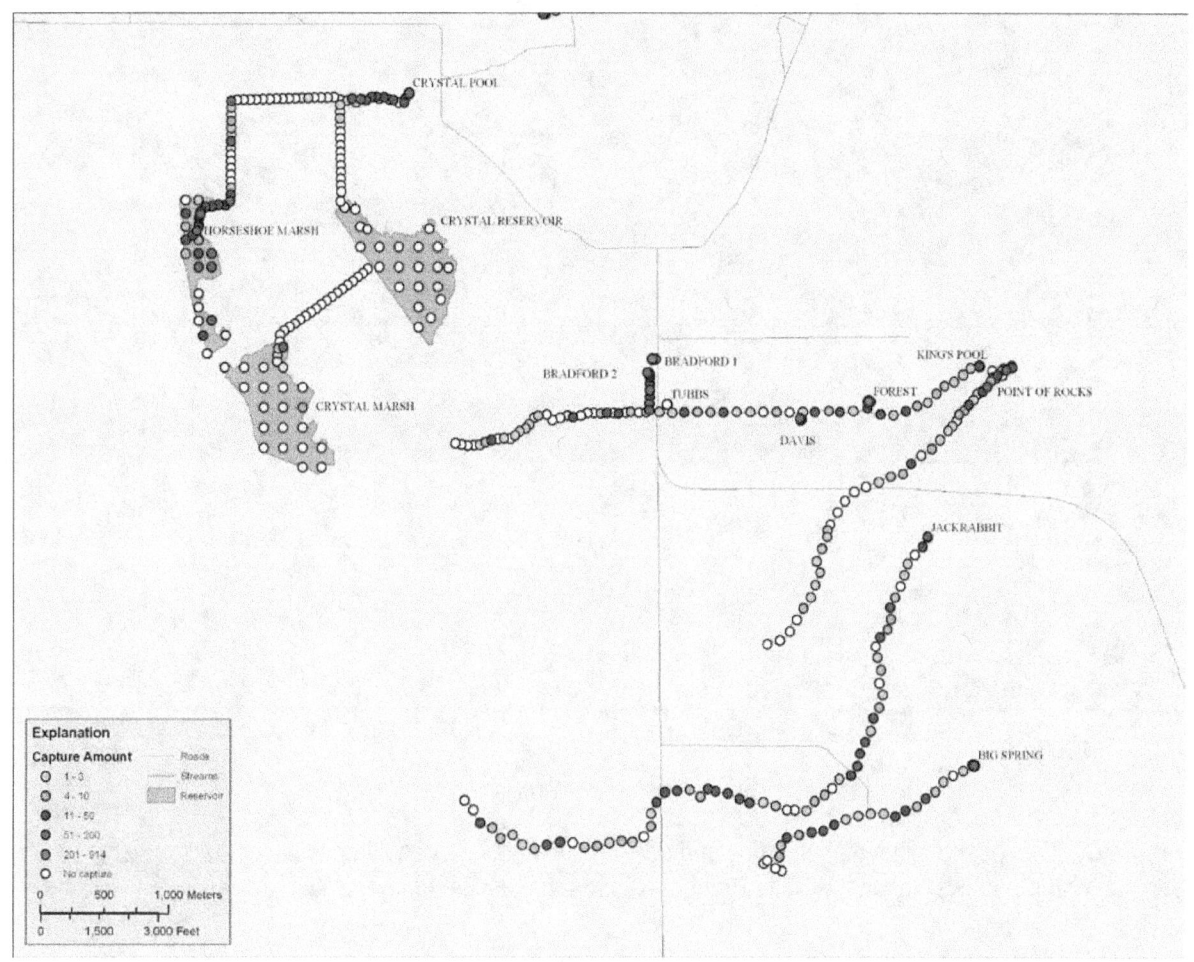

Figure C1. Composite relative abundance and seasonal distribution of mosquitofish in the southern springs, Ash Meadows National Wildlife Refuge, Nevada, fall 2007–summer 2008.

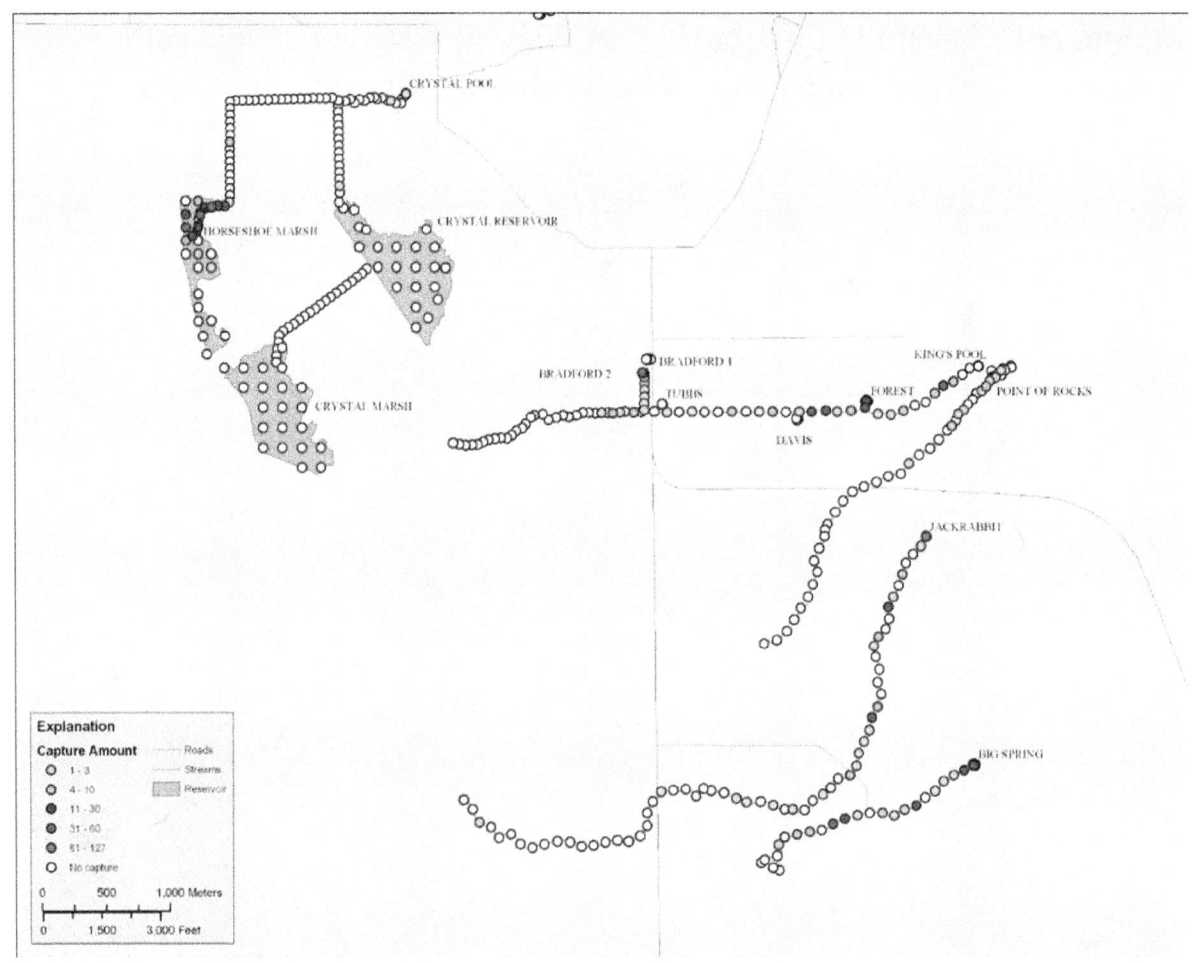

Figure C2. Composite relative abundance and seasonal distribution of salfin mollies in the southern springs, Ash Meadows National Wildlife Refuge, Nevada, fall 2007–summer 2008.

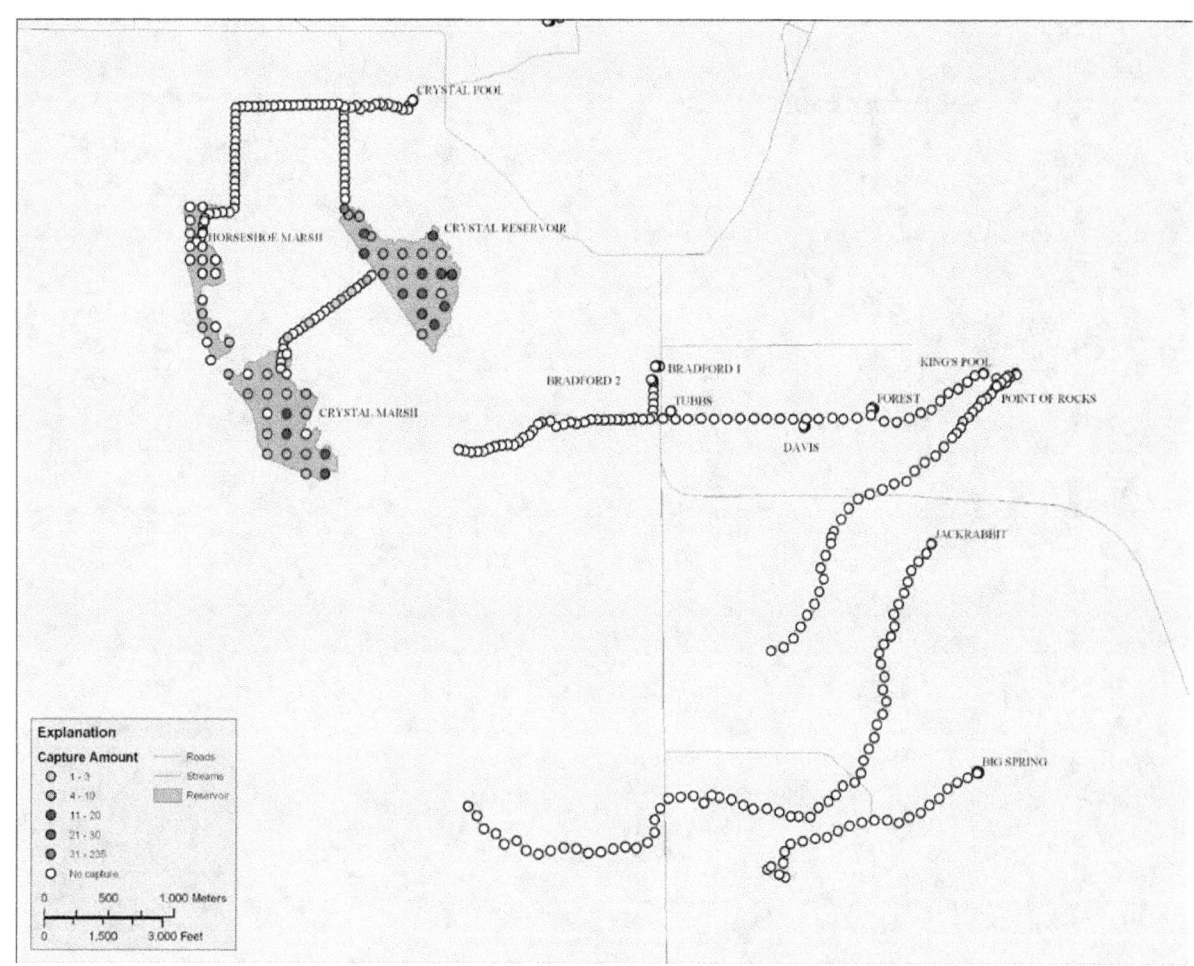

Figure C3. Composite relative abundance and seasonal distribution of green sunfish in the southern springs, Ash Meadows National Wildlife Refuge, Nevada, fall 2007–summer 2008.

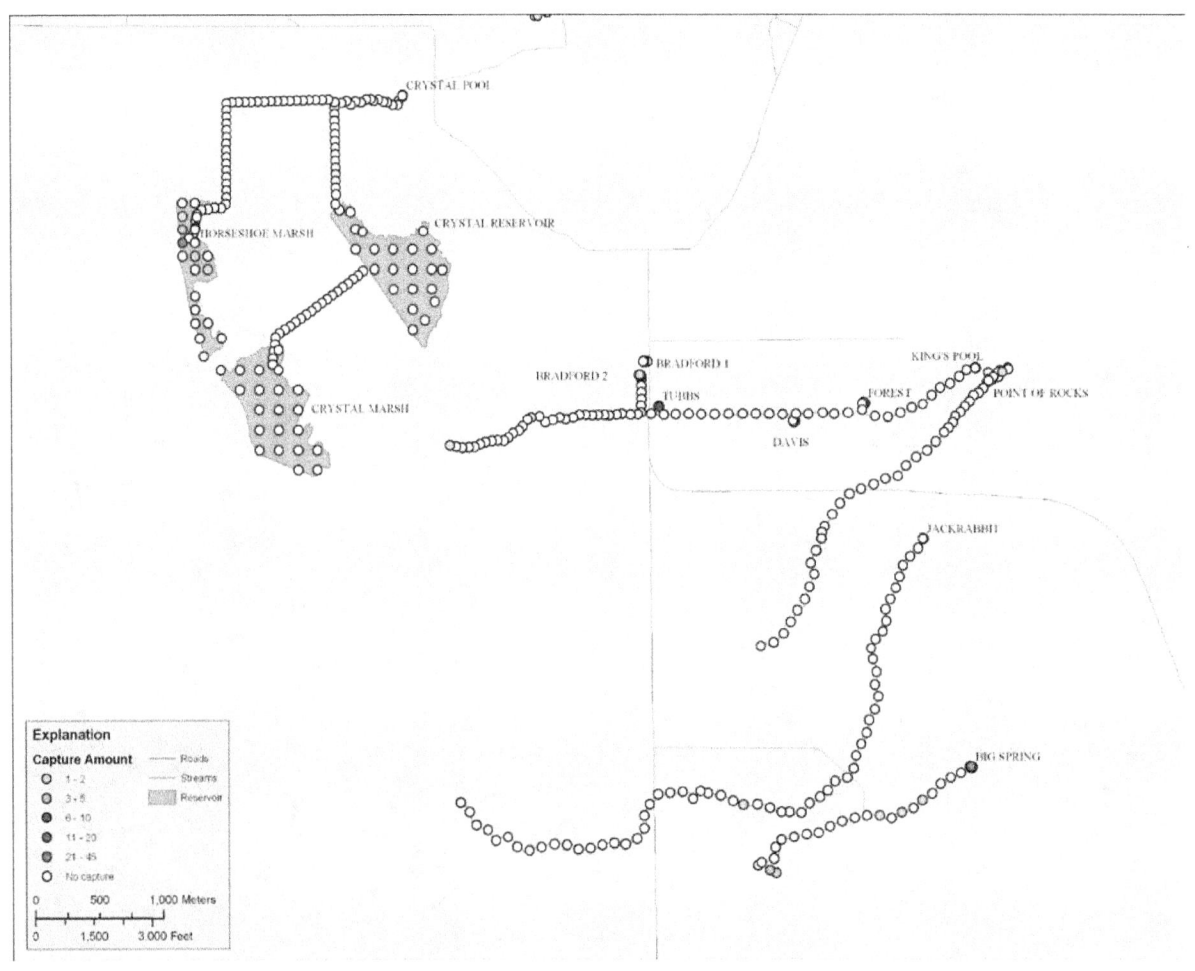

Figure C4. Composite relative abundance and seasonal distribution of bullfrogs in the southern springs, Ash Meadows National Wildlife Refuge, Nevada, fall 2007–summer 2008.

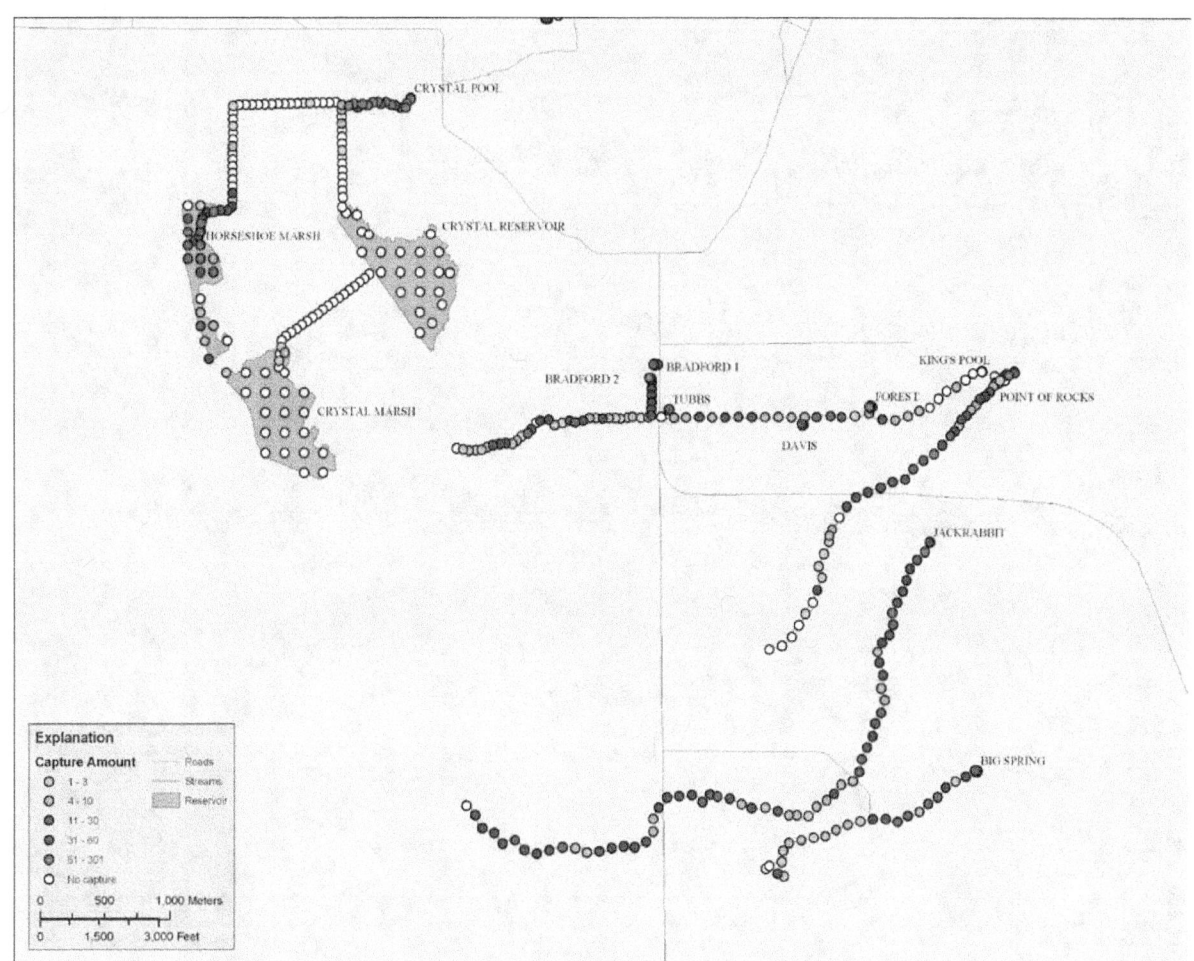

Figure C5. Composite relative abundance and seasonal distribution of crayfish in the southern springs, Ash Meadows National Wildlife Refuge, Nevada, fall 2007–summer 2008.

Table C1. Species, number, efficiency, and size captured seasonally at the southern springs of the Ash Meadows National Wildlife Refuge, Nevada.

[Spring locations are shown in figures 1 and 2. FL, fork length. Species: CYMI, Ash Meadows Amargosa pupfish; CYPE, Warm Springs Amargosa pupfish; RHON, Ash Meadows speckled dace; GAAF, Mosquitofish; POLA, Sailfin Molly; LECY, Green Sunfish; MISA, Largemouth Bass; ARNI, Convict Cichlid; AMME, Black Bullhead; LICA, Bull Frog; PRCL, Red Swamp Crayfish]

Fall 2007

System	Species	Total catch	Average/trap	n	FL (min-max)	Average ±Standard Deviation
Crystal spring-pool	CYMI	319	53.2	55	16–40	30 ±5
	GAAF	66	11.0	16	21–35	27 ±3
	POLA	1	0.2	1	40	40
	PRCL	70	11.7	38	30–68	52 ±9
Crystal stream	CYMI	1423	21.9	279	16–49	31 ±6
	GAAF	339	5.2	144	18–50	29 ±5
	POLA	105	1.6	66	17–61	33 ±8
	PRCL	609	9.4	213	15–76	55 ±10
Crystal reservoir	CYMI	–	–	–	–	–
	LECY	386	11.7	156	24–220	50 ±26
	MISA	3	0.1	3	67–91	79 ±12
Crystal stream	GAAF	1	–	1	41	41
	LECY	10	0.5	10	28–66	39 ±12
	PRCL	1	–	1	66–66	66
Crystal marsh	CYMI	24	1.1	12	16–44	28 ±7
	GAAF	66	3.1	10	19–30	26 ±3
	LECY	26	0.8	26	31–165	59 ±31
	MISA	–	–	–	–	–
	PRCL	3	0.1	3	43–48	45 ±3
Horseshoe marsh	CYMI	17	1.1	17	18–36	25 ±5
	GAAF	97	6.1	61	18–45	30 ±7
	POLA	54	3.4	30	14–55	35 ±9
	LECY	–	–	–	–	–
	LICA	1	0.1	1	150–150	150
	PRCL	210	13.1	101	27–78	58 ±11
Kings Pool spring-pool	CYMI	838	139.7	107	17–43	31 ±5
	GAAF	4	0.7	4	20–36	27 ±7
Kings Pool stream	CYMI	179	6.4	65	16–50	34 ±7
	RHON	1	.	1	51	51
	GAAF	57	2.0	52	20–47	31 ±7
	POLA	29	1.0	29	22–50	35 ±8
	PRCL	80	2.9	69	25–75	57 ±11
Point of Rocks spring-pool	CYMI	237	5.3	93	13–48	30 ±7
	RHON	–	–	–	–	–
	GAAF	29	0.6	29	23–37	29 ±4
	POLA	5	0.1	5	23–41	33 ±7
	LICA	–	–	–	–	–
	PRCL	196	4.4	150	15–70	52 ±10
Bradford 1 spring-pool	RHON	615	102.5	120	24–75	43 ±11
	GAAF	125	20.8	47	14–60	30 ±7
	PRCL	37	6.2	37	27–74	49 ±14
Bradford 1 stream	RHON	80	40.0	10	25–51	38 ±8
	GAAF	93	46.5	20	20–38	28 ±5
	PRCL	30	15.0	20	24–72	50 ±14
Bradford 2 spring-pool	RHON	31	5.2	31	29–54	43 ±5
	GAAF	358	59.7	83	18–43	26 ±5
	POLA	–	–	–	–	–
	LICA	–	–	–	–	–
	PRCL	153	25.5	89	24–65	45 ±10

Table C1. Species, number, efficiency, and size captured seasonally at the southern springs of the Ash Meadows National Wildlife Refuge, Nevada.—Continued

			Fall 2007			
System	Species	Total catch	Average/trap	n	FL (min-max)	Average ±Standard Deviation
Bradford 2 stream	CYMI	15	0.5	15	26–45	35 ±5
	RHON	95	2.9	77	28–79	46 ±9
	GAAF	163	4.9	86	19–52	36 ±7
	POLA	22	0.7	20	26–53	39 ±9
	LICA	1	–	0	–	–
	PRCL	141	4.3	125	10–75	53 ±14
Forest spring-pool	CYMI	1	0.2	1	33	33
	RHON	5	0.8	5	54–69	58 ±6
	GAAF	462	77.0	60	18–51	29 ±7
	POLA	9	1.5	9	20–47	29 ±8
	PRCL	140	23.3	50	29–89	53 ±12
Tubbs spring-pool	LICA	4	0.7	4	71–100	82 ±13
	PRCL	6	1.0	6	67–74	71 ±3
Davis spring-pool	GAAF	119	19.8	50	21–47	34 ±8
	AMME	8	1.3	8	85–97	89 ±4
	PRCL	5	0.8	5	55–75	61 ±8
Jackrabbit spring-pool	CYMI	786	131.0	55	20–55	32 ±10
	RHON	19	3.2	19	39–55	47 ±5
	GAAF	55	9.2	30	22–38	30 ±5
	POLA	69	11.5	36	18–54	35 ±10
	PRCL	25	4.2	23	30–62	44 ±10
Jackrabbit stream	CYMI	79	1.3	60	21–55	39 ±7
	RHON	510	8.5	353	22–83	50 ±12
	GAAF	121	2.0	83	21–48	33 ±7
	POLA	36	0.6	34	18–56	37 ±10
	LICA	–	–	–	–	–
	PRCL	291	4.9	199	16–72	54 ±10
Big Spring spring-pool	CYMI	157	26.2	36	13–39	25 ±6
	GAAF	2	0.3	2	21–24	23 ±2
	POLA	40	6.7	33	15–45	29 ±10
	MISA	–	–	–	–	–
	LICA	–	–	–	–	–
	PRCL	–	–	–	–	–
Big Spring stream	CYMI	253	11.5	60	22–48	35 ±7
	GAAF	14	0.6	14	25–51	32 ±8
	POLA	42	1.9	41	16–62	34 ±10
	LICA	6	0.3	6	37–55	46 ±7
	PRCL	117	5.3	97	24–73	50 ±12

Table C1. Species, number, efficiency, and size captured seasonally at the southern springs of the Ash Meadows National Wildlife Refuge, Nevada.—Continued

Winter 2008

System	Species	Total catch	Average/trap	n	FL (min-max)	Average ±Standard Deviation
Crystal spring-pool	CYMI	594	99.0	106	16–39	28 ±4
	GAAF	31	5.2	24	20–32	26 ±3
	POLA	–	–	–	–	–
	PRCL	68	11.3	68	21–53	39 ±6
Crystal stream	CYMI	1099	21.1	271	18–48	32 ±6
	GAAF	318	6.1	95	20–41	28 ±4
	POLA	17	0.3	16	24–65	37 ±10
	PRCL	639	12.3	228	22–75	49 ±10
Crystal reservoir	CYMI	–	–	–	–	–
	LECY	4	0.1	4	35–185	75 ±73
	MISA	–	–	–	–	–
Crystal stream	GAAF	–	–	–	–	–
	LECY	5	0.3	5	52–98	72 ±19
	PRCL	1	0.1	1	38	38
Crystal marsh	CYMI	14	0.7	11	16–30	25 ±4
	GAAF	5	0.3	5	21–33	29 ±5
	LECY	4	0.1	4	54–163	86 ±52
	MISA	–	–	–	–	–
	PRCL	1	0.1	1	34	34
Horseshoe marsh	CYMI	27	1.6	27	18–51	29 ±8
	GAAF	18	1.1	18	23–32	28 ±3
	POLA	34	2.0	23	25–51	37 ±7
	LECY	1	0.1	1	61	61
	LICA	11	0.6	11	41–100	79 ±15
	PRCL	81	4.8	68	25–78	54 ±13
Kings Pool spring-pool	CYMI	531	88.5	108	16–49	30 ±7
	GAAF	16	2.7	16	21–36	29 ±4
Kings Pool stream	CYMI	106	3.8	65	21–47	34 ±6
	RHON	–	–	–	–	–
	GAAF	35	1.3	35	21–50	31 ±7
	POLA	12	0.4	12	24–56	37 ±11
	PRCL	47	1.7	47	25–67	46 ±11
Point of Rocks spring-pool	CYMI	179	4.2	56	13–43	31 ±7
	RHON	5	0.1	5	43–58	51 ±6
	GAAF	91	2.1	62	16–45	30 ±6
	POLA	7	0.2	6	28–46	35 ±7
	LICA	1	–	0	–	–
	PRCL	91	2.1	85	22–65	49 ±10
Bradford 1 spring-pool	RHON	694	115.7	125	25–72	41 ±10
	GAAF	447	74.5	85	20–57	29 ±7
	PRCL	15	2.5	15	28–68	51 ±12
Bradford 1 stream	RHON	77	38.5	15	35–61	49 ±8
	GAAF	78	39.0	21	21–42	32 ±7
	PRCL	18	9.0	14	41–67	54 ±7
Bradford 2 spring-pool	RHON	9	1.5	9	41–54	47 ±5
	GAAF	390	65.0	100	18–41	27 ±4
	POLA	141	23.5	65	22–52	34 ±5
	LICA	–	–	–	–	–
	PRCL	52	8.7	47	21–67	39 ±9

Table C1. Species, number, efficiency, and size captured seasonally at the southern springs of the Ash Meadows National Wildlife Refuge, Nevada.—Continued

Winter 2008

System	Species	Total catch	Average/trap	n	FL (min-max)	Average ±Standard Deviation
Bradford 2 stream	CYMI	3	0.1	3	37–42	40 ±3
	RHON	94	2.5	70	37–80	51 ±9
	GAAF	130	3.4	87	16–52	35 ±8
	POLA	14	0.4	14	32–61	44 ±7
	LICA	1	–	1	80	80
	PRCL	100	2.6	98	18–73	50 ±15
Forest spring-pool	CYMI	2	0.3	2	39–49	44 ±7
	RHON	7	1.2	7	50–71	60 ±9
	GAAF	397	66.2	113	17–53	28 ±8
	POLA	15	2.5	15	20–45	29 ±8
	PRCL	45	7.5	44	21–75	52 ±12
Tubbs spring-pool	LICA	–	–	–	–	–
	PRCL	16	2.7	16	37–75	55 ±12
Davis spring-pool	GAAF	1	0.2	1	31	31
	AMME	–	–	–	–	–
	PRCL	4	0.7	4	50–69	62 ±9
Jackrabbit spring-pool	CYMI	726	121.0	118	18–49	31 ±7
	RHON	21	3.5	21	44–55	50 ±3
	GAAF	52	8.7	52	21–49	30 ±6
	POLA	35	5.8	27	21–42	29 ±5
	PRCL	24	4.0	24	31–66	46 ±10
Jackrabbit stream	CYMI	169	2.8	86	25–53	40 ±7
	RHON	645	10.8	405	25–82	51 ±13
	GAAF	56	0.9	51	24–55	34 ±7
	POLA	3	0.1	3	41–43	42 ±1
	LICA	–	–	–	–	–
	PRCL	295	4.9	231	15–71	44 ±13
Big Spring spring-pool	CYMI	416	69.3	89	18–42	26 ±4
	GAAF	13	2.2	13	18–27	22 ±3
	POLA	9	1.5	9	20–35	24 ±5
	MISA	–	–	–	–	–
	LICA	15	2.5	15	42–65	52 ±7
	PRCL	1	0.2	1	25–25	25
Big Spring stream	CYMI	206	9.8	70	19–55	32 ±8
	GAAF	36	1.7	36	20–51	29 ±7
	POLA	8	0.4	8	25–41	30 ±5
	LICA	14	0.7	12	35–71	55 ±12
	PRCL	92	4.4	79	28–62	45 ±9

Table C1. Species, number, efficiency, and size captured seasonally at the southern springs of the Ash Meadows National Wildlife Refuge, Nevada.—Continued

Spring 2008

System	Species	Total catch	Average/trap	n	FL (min-max)	Average ±Standard Deviation
Crystal spring-pool	CYMI	564	94.0	108	20–45	29 ±5
	GAAF	21	3.5	21	23–35	28 ±4
	POLA	2	0.3	2	36–38	37 ±1
	PRCL	24	4.0	24	39–59	49 ±5
Crystal stream	CYMI	646	17.5	241	18–52	33 ±6
	GAAF	190	5.1	108	18–47	30 ±6
	POLA	11	0.3	10	16–62	33 ±14
	PRCL	402	10.9	169	25–75	51 ±9
Crystal reservoir	CYMI	5	0.2	5	30–38	32 ±3
	LECY	9	0.3	9	38–68	52 ±9
	MISA	5	0.1	5	231–287	271 ±23
Crystal stream	GAAF	–	–	–	–	–
	LECY	–	–	–	–	–
	PRCL	–	–	–	–	–
Crystal marsh	CYMI	6	0.3	6	18–28	23 ±3
	GAAF	–	–	–	–	–
	LECY	27	0.9	27	34–175	80 ±38
	MISA	16	0.6	16	209–315	256 ±24
	PRCL	2	0.1	2	47–52	50 ±4
Horseshoe marsh	CYMI	72	4.8	30	20–42	32 ±6
	GAAF	16	1.1	16	24–39	31 ±5
	POLA	19	1.3	19	24–47	33 ±6
	LECY	5	0.3	5	64–74	70 ±4
	LICA	2	0.1	2	50–72	61 ±16
	PRCL	174	11.6	98	30–75	57 ±10
Kings Pool spring-pool	CYMI	653	108.8	108	18–44	29 ±6
	GAAF	1	0.2	1	34	34
Kings Pool stream	CYMI	170	6.1	93	28–51	35 ±5
	RHON	–	–	–	–	–
	GAAF	29	1.0	29	19–44	30 ±7
	POLA	29	1.0	26	20–41	33 ±5
	PRCL	78	2.8	73	33–71	54 ±10
Point of Rocks spring-pool	CYMI	227	5.5	152	17–44	31 ±6
	RHON	2	–	2	38–65	52 ±19
	GAAF	49	1.2	42	20–47	31 ±5
	POLA	6	0.1	6	32–42	38 ±3
	LICA	–	–	–	–	–
	PRCL	148	3.6	112	19–73	52 ±12
Bradford 1 spring-pool	RHON	383	63.8	100	37–72	46 ±7
	GAAF	51	8.5	46	20–45	34 ±7
	PRCL	29	4.8	29	32–70	50 ±11
Bradford 1 stream	RHON	–	–	–	–	–
	GAAF	261	130.5	21	24–60	35 ±9
	PRCL	13	6.5	10	42–70	59 ±8
Bradford 2 spring-pool	RHON	–	–	–	–	–
	GAAF	–	–	–	–	–
	POLA	–	–	–	–	–
	LICA	1	0.2	0	–	–
	PRCL	95	15.8	68	26–68	44 ±10

Table C1. Species, number, efficiency, and size captured seasonally at the southern springs of the Ash Meadows National Wildlife Refuge, Nevada.—Continued

Spring 2008

System	Species	Total catch	Average/trap	n	FL (min-max)	Average ±Standard Deviation
Bradford 2 stream	CYMI	14	0.4	14	25–42	33 ±5
	RHON	79	2.1	57	31–79	48 ±10
	GAAF	88	2.3	61	20–52	35 ±6
	POLA	1	–	1	35	35
	LICA	2	0.1	2	71–101	86 ±21
	PRCL	85	2.2	85	21–75	54 ±12
Forest spring-pool	CYMI	55	9.2	55	32–57	42 ±6
	RHON	7	1.2	7	42–70	54 ±9
	GAAF	287	47.8	83	16–47	28 ±7
	POLA	1	0.2	1	37	37
	PRCL	152	25.3	110	17–68	49 ±10
Tubbs spring-pool	LICA	2	0.3	2	105–115	110 ±7
	PRCL	49	8.2	49	20–74	54 ±10
Davis spring-pool	GAAF	359	59.8	112	22–53	38 ±7
	AMME	2	0.3	2	95–103	99 ±6
	PRCL	19	3.2	19	28–73	47 ±14
Jackrabbit spring-pool	CYMI	761	126.8	120	16–53	31 ±7
	RHON	31	5.2	31	42–60	50 ±5
	GAAF	1	0.2	1	40	40
	POLA	75	12.5	66	16–55	38 ±6
	PRCL	19	3.2	19	31–66	47 ±9
Jackrabbit stream	CYMI	176	2.9	126	21–54	38 ±7
	RHON	659	11.0	440	28–85)	51 ±11
	GAAF	91	1.5	65	20–60	36 ±8
	POLA	8	0.1	8	25–44	37 ±6
	LICA	1	–	0	–	–
	PRCL	288	4.8	231	15–77	52 ±11
Big Spring spring-pool	CYMI	107	17.8	67	15–34	23 ±4
	GAAF	5	0.8	5	21–25	23 ±1
	POLA	5	0.8	5	18–28	25 ±4
	MISA	10	–	8	235–365	277 ±43
	LICA	–	–	–	–	–
	PRCL	–	–	–	–	–
Big Spring stream	CYMI	117	6.2	61	17–51	30 ±7
	GAAF	30	1.6	30	5–44	32 ±8
	POLA	18	0.9	18	13–49	32 ±12
	LICA	–	–	–	–	–
	PRCL	120	6.3	75	31–67	52 ±9

Table C1. Species, number, efficiency, and size captured seasonally at the southern springs of the Ash Meadows National Wildlife Refuge, Nevada.—Continued

			Summer 2008			
System	Species	Total catch	Average/trap	n	FL (min-max)	Average ±Standard Deviation
Crystal spring-pool	CYMI	554	92.3	103	22–46	32 ±5
	GAAF	27	4.5	25	17–41	29 ±7
	POLA	–	–	–	–	–
	PRCL	34	5.7	34	41–72	56 ±7
Crystal stream	CYMI	958	36.8	225	14–51	30 ±7
	GAAF	242	9.3	96	18–48	29 ±7
	POLA	3	0.1	3	22–35	29 ±7
	PRCL	605	23.3	150	35–72	56 ±8
Crystal reservoir	CYMI	–	–	–	–	–
	LECY	77	2.6	77	18–216	62 ±32
	MISA	–	–	–	–	–
Crystal stream	GAAF	–	–	–	–	–
	LECY	–	–	–	–	–
	PRCL	–	–	–	–	–
Crystal marsh	CYMI	4	0.5	4	22–28	24 ±3
	GAAF	4	0.5	4	17–23	20 ±3
	LECY	41	3.7	39	16–167	46 ±37
	MISA	1	0.1	1	48	48
	PRCL	–	–	–	–	–
Horseshoe marsh	CYMI	12	1.2	12	26–40	35 ±5
	GAAF	437	43.7	78	16–68	26 ±8
	POLA	44	4.4	11	21–42	33 ±7
	LECY	–	–	–	–	–
	LICA	37	3.7	0	–	–
	PRCL	162	16.2	69	29–72	54 ±11
Kings Pool spring-pool	CYMI	701	116.8	100	16–46	32 ±6
	GAAF	2	0.3	2	32–33	33 ±1
Kings Pool stream	CYMI	157	5.6	96	23–49	36 ±6
	RHON	–	–	–	–	–
	GAAF	74	2.6	69	15–51	33 ±7
	POLA	41	1.5	31	21–49	34 ±7
	PRCL	104	3.7	92	29–72	56 ±9
Point of Rocks spring-pool	CYMI	234	5.9	130	15–45	31 ±5
	RHON	–	–	–	–	–
	GAAF	119	3.0	96	18–45	30 ±6
	POLA	3	0.1	3	29–37	32 ±4
	LICA	–	–	–	–	–
	PRCL	198	5.0	156	17–75	53 ±12
Bradford 1 spring-pool	RHON	265	44.2	78	34–62	49 ±6
	GAAF	334	55.7	88	18–56	30 ±10
	PRCL	29	4.8	29	29–78	53 ±14
Bradford 1 stream	RHON	33	8.3	14	50–62	55 ±3
	GAAF	692	173.0	40	21–55	31 ±9
	PRCL	26	6.5	26	30–71	55 ±11
Bradford 2 spring-pool	RHON	2	0.3	2	33–42	38 ±6
	GAAF	31	5.2	30	18–46	25 ±5
	POLA	–	–	–	–	–
	LICA	–	–	–	–	–
	PRCL	40	6.7	40	25–60	46 ±9

Table C1. Species, number, efficiency, and size captured seasonally at the southern springs of the Ash Meadows National Wildlife Refuge, Nevada.—Continued

Summer 2008

System	Species	Total catch	Average/trap	n	FL (min-max)	Average ±Standard Deviation
Bradford 2 stream	CYMI	5	0.1	5	22–41	30 ±8
	RHON	78	2.1	55	27–74	47 ±11
	GAAF	123	3.3	79	20–51	35 ±7
	POLA	4	0.1	4	21–40	31 ±8
	LICA	–	–	–	–	–
	PRCL	120	3.2	117	21–71	54 ±11
Forest spring-pool	CYMI	42	5.3	42	27–54	41 ±7
	RHON	1	0.1	1	55	55
	GAAF	415	51.9	141	12–45	26 ±6
	POLA	4	0.5	4	16–50	33 ±14
	PRCL	140	17.5	114	25–71	51 ±10
Tubbs spring-pool	LICA	8	1.3	0	–	–
	PRCL	51	8.5	51	20-78	52 ±13
Davis spring-pool	GAAF	–	–	–	–	–
	AMME	–	–	–	–	–
	PRCL	11	1.8	11	35–58	45 ±8
Jackrabbit spring-pool	CYMI	512	85.3	112	17–48	34 ±7
	RHON	23	3.8	23	44–58	50 ±4
	GAAF	28	4.7	28	18–46	32 ±9
	POLA	32	5.3	32	17–49	29 ±8
	PRCL	43	7.2	43	25–72	51 ±10
Jackrabbit stream	CYMI	147	2.5	135	15–54	36 ±9
	RHON	607	10.1	413	21–91	55 ±12
	GAAF	333	5.6	253	20–56	32 ±7
	POLA	11	0.2	11	22–45	33 ±8
	LICA	–	–	–	–	–
	PRCL	461	7.7	356	27–74	55 ±10
Big Spring spring-pool	CYMI	213	35.5	76	7–32	21 ±4
	GAAF	128	21.3	50	10–31	21 ±4
	POLA	32	5.3	32	11–33	23 ±6
	MISA	–	–	–	–	–
	LICA	8	1.3	0	–	–
	PRCL	7	1.2	7	43–65	59 ±7
Big Spring stream	CYMI	61	3.2	61	18–42	30 ±6
	GAAF	109	5.7	83	18–45	30 ±7
	POLA	44	2.3	35	18–65	30 ±11
	LICA	2	0.1	2	58–60	59 ±1
	PRCL	54	2.8	54	30–75	54 ±11